DATE DUE

9/3I∠∠			
	45-230		Printed in USA

Savages
Shakespeare Wallah

James Ivory

"Savages"

a film by James Ivory from a
screenplay by George Swift Trow
and Michael O'Donoghue

"Shakespeare Wallah"

a film by James Ivory from a
screenplay by R. Prawer Jhabvala
and James Ivory

Grove Press Inc, New York

ISBN: 0-394-17799-1

Library of Congress Catalog Card Number: 73-5503

Manufactured in Great Britain
by Highbury Press Ltd.

Cover photograph by Fred Ohringer

First Evergreen Edition, 1973

First Printing

Distributed by Random House, Inc., New York

Contents

Beechwood, Scarborough, New York

Introduction
James Ivory

My accidental discovery of Beechwood, a neo-Georgian mansion in Scarborough, New York, led to the making of *Savages,* though at the time—November, 1970—I couldn't have described what sort of a film I wanted to shoot in it. There was something a bit unearthly in the ambience of Beechwood, something poetic, which made it unlike other houses of the kind I'd seen in America, and this strangeness made me think sometimes of a kind of Hudson River *Last Year at Marienbad.* To walk through the series of ever-grander rooms strung out in a line starting at the rather poky eighteenth century core is to receive a lesson in American domestic architecture over the years, but it is more of a lesson on a society which has now completely disappeared. The heyday of Beechwood was from the Nineties until the American depression. It is exactly the kind of place Scott Fitzgerald went to big parties in and wrote about. He would have understood the mentality of the family that created it: energetic Midwesterners named Vanderlip who made a lot of money out of the railroads and who wanted to put on a bit of a show. Today, with its somewhat derelict look, it has the air of a fashionable, run-down Westchester asylum—good material for another American writer, John Cheever, who once lived in a cottage on the grounds.

The idea for *Savages* sprang nearly fully-formed out of a conversation—mainly frivolous—with George Swift Trow, a young staff writer on the *New Yorker,* who had been collaborating with me on a screenplay. It was one of those projects which starts out as ". . . Wouldn't it be fun if . . ." but usually never gets carried forward. I had in mind at first a kind of *Exterminating Angel* in reverse, in which a band of primitive people becomes rapidly civilised and then reverts equally rapidly to its original state. It was Michael O'Donoghue of the *National Lampoon,* called in by Trow to collaborate on the script with him, who thought up the device of the fateful croquet ball, and it was Trow who firmly set the story within the confines of one day—from dawn to dawn—during a weekend house party.

One might think that it would not have been easy to get the money for such a peculiar project, but we got it in one day, for which I can thank the enthusiasm of the producer and that of Joseph Saleh, who backed an earlier film of ours, *Bombay Talkie*. Shooting began (with a non-union crew) eight weeks after getting Saleh's go-ahead and we finished in $37\frac{1}{2}$ days. The negative cost was under four hundred thousand dollars and I hope I'll be forgiven if I say I think that *Savages* looks like a more expensive film. Much of this is due to Walter Lassally, the cameraman. While I am thanking those who were responsible for what must seem like the ultimate directorial indulgence, I would like to express my gratitude to David Swope, Jr., who first took me to Beechwood, and to his parents, Mr. and Mrs. David Swope, Sr., who helped us in many, many ways, and, finally, to the Schoales family.

Savages was thought of as a charade meant to illustrate a serious theme: the rise and fall of civilisation. But one can imagine it too as a sort of old-fashioned textbook of the kind once used in American high schools, with steel engraved illustrations and here and there a colour plate to emphasise the high points: *Trow and O'Donoghue's Ancient History*; we put in the untitled excerpts from Schiller and Heine in order to create an atmosphere suggestive of deep scholarly endeavour. We had no special past civilisation in mind: Egypt, Rome, India, the present day—each of these offered plenty of good material; probably as much that is relevant to our theme has been left out as put in. With such a premise—a band of primitives led to an old house by a croquet ball, where they go through a profound cultural metamorphosis—it didn't seem possible to adopt a realistic story-telling style. Instead, a series of tableaux have been strung together, each one meant to be read as a point along a rising or falling curve, and it is in the viewer's recognition of these stages of advance and decay as the houseparty moves from event to event that a lot of the fun is to be found. That, at any rate, was our hope, without becoming too serious about it all.

Beechwood was a time capsule, sealed at the end of the Thirties by the Second World War, when the Vanderlip men went into the services and the staff left—one imagines—for the war plants. Nothing was ever changed after that, so we put our savages into the clothes of that decade, which also removed them from a too-familiar present with its own associations. Strangely, the actual shooting of the film became a *coup de grace* to whatever remained of the spirit of the house, for the requirements of our work were to disturb forever what was still intact of a family nature. We entered rooms which had been sealed up for a decade or more and which were still pervaded powerfully by the presence of the men and women who had once lived in them—people, moreover, who had very carefully guarded the mementoes of a lifetime: heaps of letters, photographs, newspaper clippings, pressed corsages, locks of baby hair, lists of debutantes, old cheque books. Who was to care for these things now? In fact, the last member of the Vanderlip family to live at Beechwood, a grandson of the man who enlarged it so splendidly, gave up camping there with his wife and dogs while we were shooting and went to live for good in another house nearby. Once he had gone the house became—and quite obviously—just a shell; we felt the woods could so easily move in on it, that vines would creep over the window sills, and that the ghost of a murderer said to lurk in the place would really move in and roam about dragging his shackles.

(Portions of the above appeared in a somewhat different form in *Sight and Sound,* Autumn 1971.)

A Motion Picture Treatment
James Ivory, George Swift Trow, Michael O'Donoghue

1. *Dawn in a forest.* Pale light in the sky. Woods indistinct. Rustling of leaves, sound of soft, wooden whistles. On a sort of bluff or ledge of stone elevated above the rest there is seen a cloud of smoke drifting up into the sky or trees. The camera reveals the source of smoke—a small fire, banked with damp leaves. It holds on this. Suddenly more leaves are scattered on the fire from beyond the range of the camera, and then several pairs of naked feet are seen. They are caked and painted with a mixture of mud and ash. The feet do a little shuffling step at the edge of the fire—up and down, up and down. The camera pulls back and we see there are more than a dozen men and women, daubed all over with the mud and ash. They wear masks. They lean over the fire inhaling the smoke, which has a narcotic effect. These "mud people" communicate with each other by means of little wooden whistles. They make a soft, tooting kind of tone.

2. *Slightly later.* The mudmen move along a trail in the forest. They lead one of their members towards a clearing. His wrists are tied with vines and his mask has markings on it to set him apart. The mudmen signal with their whistles and answering whistles from the woods indicate someone is coming to meet them. The mudmen become excited and all start whistling as three or four more come out of the brush. The most important of these is a woman—the Priestess—her mask is painted with designs. She seems to be in command and is deferred to by the others; yet when she comes up to them, a curious thing happens: she turns her back and leans over in a waiting, expectant position. The mudman whose wrists have been tied is led over to the woman. He seizes her and the others in the group close in around them. They have been blowing their whistles up to this point. Now they stop. They continue their shuffling dance step in silence.

3. *Later still*. The mudman whose wrists have been tied stands alone in the clearing, waiting. The others approach him and remove his mask, but the face underneath is as smeared with ash as the rest of his body. He lies down on the ground, resting his head on a flat stone. He does this as automatically as when he went up to the Priestess in the previous scene to seize her. It is clear that this man—The "Consort"—is about to be sacrificed, as the others gather around him in a threatening circle. Picking up an enormous rock or tree trunk, they hold it over his head, waiting for a signal from the Priestess to drop it. She stands apart from and above the rest of the tribe, emphasising her power. She looks towards the east, waiting for the sun. The sky is very red and the edge of the sun appears on the horizon. But before she can give her signal, a croquet ball, bright red and "special", rolls into the clearing, through the circle, and strikes the sacrificial stone with a sharp click, the click of two croquet balls. The ritual is interrupted. Frantic whistling . . . perhaps piercing staccato bursts. Everyone but the Priestess runs into the woods; she, however, comes forward to claim the croquet ball. After she examines it, she gives one long whistle which is different from any we've heard and the mudmen reappear. An Old Man shows the Priestess from which direction the ball came. She confers with the Leader and they set off in that direction. Others follow, some slowly, some reluctantly. . . . Their order indicates tribal status: Leader first, followed by the Violent Man. The rest of the men surround and protect the Priestess. The Eternal Slut is the last to leave. The Poet-Consort is left standing alone in the clearing . . . the whistles get more and more faint.

4. *Forest Trail*. As the tribe proceeds through the forest, there is foraging for edibles—bugs, berries, etc. A disturbance in the underbrush alerts the mudmen. They spot some creature moving away from them and they go after it. The creature is a brown-skinned, lithe girl whom they stalk and capture after a short chase. Terrified of the mudmen, she fights back, but finally is subdued. She wears a string of bright blue beads around her waist. The mudmen return to the trail and their search for the source of the croquet ball. The Man-Woman is fascinated by the Forest Girl's blue beads. He makes her give them to him and he puts them around his neck. He gives her a branch to cover her nakedness. The tribe moves on and down into the little valley which is very dense with growth. Someone finds a croquet mallet leaning against a tree and brings it to the Priestess. After going further, they reach a grassy area where someone trips over a croquet wicket. Curious, they investigate and come upon overgrown statuary, a rotting arbor, etc. There is an almost-empty wine glass in this arbor. Flies crawl on it.

5. *The Swimming Pool*. They discover an empty swimming pool and kneeling, lap the puddle of brackish water at the bottom. Some remove their masks and leave them by the pool. Faint "Jazz Baby" music played backwards. There is a skeleton in dinner clothes lying in the pool, obscured by leaves and overgrowth. The Limping Man is drawn to it, stares for a moment, then passes on.

6. *The Motor Car*. The tribe comes upon a vintage motor car. A shoe or article of ancient lingerie is in the back seat. While investigating, someone accidently bumps the horn. The sound is feeble, the sound of a car that has not been used for years. The mudmen vanish into the foliage. The Leader is the first to re-emerge. With the Violent Man and the other men, he cautiously approaches the car and examines it. Perhaps he tries the horn. The tribe then gathers flowers and strews them on the car, hoping to placate whatever spirit inhabits it.

7. *The House*. During the above, the Child enters the house, walking past the camera, which is inside. The mudmen go in search of her, and the camera pulls back, revealing walls, furniture, and vistas of other rooms, all uninhabited. This is the first time the viewer knows there is a house. In the background, the tribe notes the disappearance of the Girl and crowds around the doorway afraid to enter. Finally, the Old Couple, who watch over the Child, enter the house. It is significant that the Old Couple lead the search as they're motivated by affection, not tribal authority. After them comes the limping man, the Leader, the Priestess (still holding the croquet ball), the Violent Man, the Misanthropic Woman, the Man-Woman, the Unstable Girl, etc. The Eternal Slut stays outside. She blows her whistle, hoping to bring the others back.

8. *Rooms*. Confronted with civilisation, the mud people investigate the house, in roughly the following order: Entrance through sunroom; through darkened panelled room past a film projector; through hallway near landing, where they hesitate; through dining room, where there are the remains of a dinner; through collection room with its paintings, cabinets, and other objects, to library. The Man-Woman, intrigued by the collections, stays behind after the others have moved on. He stares at a portrait fixedly. He licks the portrait.

9. *Birth of Religion*. The mudmen pull open some tall doors leading into the octagonal library. They fall back in fear and wonder at what they see. A life-size statue of Minerva, golden and illuminated by a shaft of sunlight, stands above them. The Priestess enters, places the croquet ball before the statue. The mudmen watch her in awe. She

turns them out of the room and closes the door.

10. *The Photograph Album.* The Consort-Poet finds an old velvet-bound book of photographs but the subjects of the photographs are missing: All that is left in the photographs is a shoe on an ottoman or a cork-tipped cigarette smouldering in an ashtray, as if a person stepped out of the frame just before the picture was taken. He studies these pictures. The Eternal Slut knocks on the glass to get his attention, but doesn't succeed.

11. *The Huddle.* Despite minor frictions (fighting over shiny objects —i.e., doorknobs, with the Priestess acting as arbiter) the mud people huddle together in the house. Some engage in communal hygiene (picking off lice from other's hair, etc.). The Poet-Consort approaches and cautiously joins the huddle. The Eternal Slut finally comes inside. She too joins the huddle. As yet, no one has ventured upstairs.

12. *The Swimming Pool.* The mud people find that the swimming pool has been inexplicably filled. They go for a swim and some of their mud is washed off in the process. The Eternal Slut, eternally on the fringes of civilised society, calls from the underbrush. At the shallow end of the pool, the Child swims while the Limping Man, who cannot swim, consciously washes his mud off. While playing in the water, one of the Young Lovers caresses the other's back, as if discovering it for the first time.

13. *The Mirror.* At last the mudmen climb the stairs to the second floor. In climbing the stairs, they encounter an enormous mirror which reflects their images, frightening them. They shout—the first human sound so far. They gather behind the Priestess who throws her croquet ball at the mirror, shattering it. The ball returns down the stairs to her in a curious, controlled fashion. The Poet-Consort picks it up. The Priestess takes it away and they go upstairs.

14. *Clothes.* The mud people, led by the Misanthropic Woman, discover clothes in the bedroom closets. They pull them out and examine them closely and some of them put the clothes on, although, in most cases, incorrectly. At first, men's and women's garments are interchangeable, but finally they are put on right; shoes, stockings, gloves, hats, underwear—these things remain mysterious and intriguing. Nor has all the mud been washed off: muddy arms, muddy feet, plus a few people still entirely covered with mud (the Eternal Slut). We see the individuality—the faces and expressions—of the individual mudmen, up to now hidden, emerge. Yet the mud and grime is still pronounced. The mudmen go off to other rooms, wearing or merely carrying, the clothes. The Man-Woman, who is clearly male, stays

behind. He-She looks carefully at all the things which have turned up, trying some, discarding others. He ends up choosing dress appropriate for a woman.

15. *Speech.* Speech is starting, like that of sweet, bright children. With speech, also begin simple personal relationships, having to do with individuals and not with group or tribal feelings.

16. *Separate actions.* The group consciousness is beginning to break down, despite the Priestess who tries to hold it together. She continually tries to dominate by virtue of her assumption of high-priestly powers and in some instances is successful, but her influence wanes as individual prerogatives increase. The mudmen begin assuming not only personalities but identities as to function within the house.

17. *The Croquet Game.* The Misanthropic Woman, the Violent Man, the Limping Man, and the Unstable Girl begin playing a lighthearted game of croquet. (These four are usually in advance of the others. . . .) The rest join them and they have a sweet, joyous garden party. Asha serves lemonade, as instructed by the Priestess, whom we see has now become a society matron. All are dressed properly. Towards twilight, a dead whippet is found on the pavement. While the four continue to play croquet, the others gather around it in a circle, somewhat automatically, as if for some ritual that they've forgotten. As the Priestess-Society Matron steps forward, uncertain, hesitant, but knowing that something is necessary, all the lights in the house go on behind them. The sun has set. They drift across the lawn and up the paths. They make polite small talk.

18. *Dinner.* A fine dinner has been laid with two caviar-filled swans carved out of ice. As the mud people file in, one notes that they're perfectly dressed for dinner, the men in tuxedos, the women in long dresses and jewels. The mood is Victorian. The conversation is elegant and witty. Everyone has a name now, yet no one has changed. The Eternal Slut is overdressed and still appealing to be liked; the Leader talks of boring banker's topics like embargoes and interest on municipal bonds; the Poet alternates between becoming silences and bursts of talk; the Unstable Girl is charmingly unstable, making remarks the meaning of which are not entirely clear; the Violent Man, within the decorum of the dinner party as set by the Priestess, contradicts his table partners; the Misanthropic Woman backbites and tries flirtation; the Limping Man says wise things, to which the Poet and the Unstable Girl pay close attention; the Old Couple reminisce; the Man-Woman firmly leads the conversation to uplifting and educational topics. Presiding over all this is the Priestess-Hostess. She has separated the Young Lovers, so that the young man sits between the

Misanthropic Lady and the Unstable Girl, and his beloved is put next to the Violent Man and the Poet. They grow used to this separation. The Forest Girl has no place at the table. She has become a ladies' maid. The Man-Woman speaks of primitive tribes and savage fertility rites as one who has read an ever-so-interesting article in the *National Geographic*. What particularly interests her, she says, is the odd custom of murdering the Consort of the tribal Priestess. The others agree that this is indeed a strange custom. In the midst of dinner, all stop talking as if caught in a prolonged and mysterious silence which they cannot beak . . . we hear the sound of rustling trees. Unnoticed, the croquet ball rolls across the floor, through the room, down the stairs, and heads toward the croquet court. When it has gone, conversation continues.

19. *The Sinking of the LUSITANIA*. The women withdraw to the French Room, leaving the men alone to talk, over brandy, about hints of the coming warfare. The men join the ladies, but before they can socialise, the radio comes on. All freeze. The announcer is describing the sinking of an ocean liner (actually the LUSITANIA, but never mentioned). When he tells how, from his vantage point, he can see the ship struck by a torpedo, the chandelier sounds a tinkling tremor, although no motion is discernible. When he tells how the lifeboats are lowered, how some capsize and how men leap from the decks of the listing ship, no one moves. Everyone's attention is rivetted. Finally, he says, "And now, I can see this great old queen of the sea, with all her lights ablaze, commencing to sink beneath the waves. . . ." (The voice fades in and out, broken by static.) From a great distance we see the house, with all its lights ablaze. No motion. Just the voice fading in and out, describing the ship as it goes under. When the ship has sunk, the radio goes dead. Silence. The Old Man goes to the piano and plays and sings "Follow the Gleam". Others join in as an act of courage until they're all singing. After a few choruses, they hum, underscoring terse dialogue.

20. *Low key scene*. Young Lovers carrying on a mild flirtation with other partners.

21. *Gaiety*. The Misanthropic Woman, waving an ostrich feather fan, puts on some kind of Cole Porter "Steppin' on the Spaniel" type phonograph music. At this point, the mood turns gayer. Action becomes fragmented. Two people play parchesi. Some dance. The pace quickens. Champagne is splashed about. A silent movie projector shows a film of what seems to be a black musical or revue of the late 20's, intercut with shots of a magician opening a large box. However, just when something is to be revealed, the film breaks down.

When it is rethreaded, the film starts in at an earlier point, builds up to the same climax, and breaks down again. The mudmen, in their evening clothes, are intrigued by the film.

22. *Poolside.* At the pool, where strings of coloured lights and lanterns have been hung up, the party has reached F. Scott Fitzgerald atmosphere: squirting champagne, wild dancing, uncontrollable laughter, etc. In the madness, the Limping Man is knocked or shoved into the pool. As he drowns, the poolside party goes on. No one notices him. Or, the others pretend not to notice him . . . he sinks slowly, making no sound.

23. *Charades.* Charades are suggested. The dancing stops and all leave for the house where they are still trying to get the film in the projector past the "revelation", but, like a recurring dream, that point is never reached. Only the Child is left by the pool. The charades show what has become of the mudmen's relationships. For example, the Priestess and the Poet-Consort feel they have some special attraction for each other: What is it? Everyone's speech as they try to guess the subject of the charades becomes very mannered: style is replacing feelings.

24. *The Game.* Dialogue turns very odd. Someone cuts his bare foot on mirror fragments at the top of the stairs. A strange game is played in which one person is "it" and the others shout out numbers: "43" (a man crawls about the floor on all fours, licking the air); "15" (Asha, readmitted to the company, lies over a chair); someone kneels in a curious position on a table when a number is called, but gets down when the caller says, "I said '77' not '67'!" In the dining room, the swans have melted into shapeless and indecipherable forms.

25. *The Japanese Room.* Re-emergence of the Narcotic Leaf: Some go to the Japanese Room where they take the narcotic leaf. The Child assists in the preparation. Many involved in this have changed into occult robes. Buddhist chant . . . Oriental rites. Asha, still in her maid's outfit, is the leader of these activities.

26. *Decay.* Everything is coming apart fast. Even the Old Couple have betrayed each other. Freaky sex. Clothing begins to disappear. The Misanthropic Woman starts speaking French. She and some of the others have painted their faces white. . . . They roam about the place. No one notices that the film in the projector has gone past the breakdown point at last, and the "mystery" is revealed, if they would only care to watch.

27. *The Motor Car*. The interior is lit. The Forest Girl and the Misanthropic Woman sit in the back seat with arms around each other. They discuss removal of body hair (diathermy, etc.). They turn the headlights on revealing the Unstable Girl hanging. . . .

28. *Croquet*. The sky is getting light. The Misanthropic Woman stops speaking French. The lights in the house flicker and go out. The projector stops. The phonograph stops. The Poet-Consort picks up a record and looks at it curiously. He holds it next to his ear. The Violent Man snatches it away and holds it next to *his* ear. Still nothing. He smashes the record. Then he smashes all the records in sight. From inside one can see the ocean outside the windows. The mud people are drawn to the lawn . . . some in dinner clothes, some in lingerie. They begin to play croquet. It rains slightly and they catch raindrops on their tongues. The lawn is wet. Many remove their shoes. The Leader eats a bug from a bush. The Man-Woman has a 5 o'clock shadow by now and is abandoning her clothes, turning back into a man. Perhaps she wears only a skirt, looking like a Polynesian warrior. Names are forgotten. Sentences begin but don't end: "I read the most interesting . . . uh . . . uh . . . aaah. . . ." The Priestess-Hostess, idly trailing her hand in a flower bed at one point, gets some mud on her fingers and unthinkingly spreads it over the back of her hand . . . "it feels so nice and cool", she tells the others. The Eternal Slut flirts with the man of the Young Lovers and tries to lure him into the woods. She sends his croquet ball into the woods and then hits her own after it. They disappear into the leaves. Others send the balls of their opponents into the woods and are sent themselves. The Violent Man and the Priestess have a last glass of wine in the arbor and then enter the forest. Only the Poet-Consort is left. He is playing the red "special" ball. He still wears dinner dress, though his bare feet are muddy.

29. *Shots throughout the house*. Pulling away . . . room by darkened room. The dawn light comes in through the windows . . . pulling away. A shot of the swimming pool where the Limping Man lies at the bottom covered with leaves, the water having mysteriously drained out. Whistles are calling to the Poet-Consort. Rustling tree sounds. He hesitates, looks about. He is all alone on the lawn. The abandoned house looms behind him. Very consciously, making a choice apparently, he hits his own ball exactly as the sun rises. It flies into the woods and he follows it. The sun comes up.

Credits

Angelika Films presents
in association with Merchant Ivory Productions
Savages
starring
Louis Stadlen as Julian Branch, a song writer
Anne Francine as Carlotta, a hostess
Thayer David as Otto Nürder, a capitalist
Susie Blakely as Cecily, a debutante
Russ Thacker as Andrew, an eligible young man
Salome Jens as Emily Penning, a woman in disgrace
Margaret Brewster as Lady Cora
Neil Fitzgerald as Sir Harry
Eva Saleh as Zia, the child
Ultra Violet as Iliona, a decadent
Asha Puthli as the Forest Girl
Martin Kove as Archie, a bully
Kathleen Widdoes as Leslie
Christopher Pennock as Hester
Sam Waterston as James, the limping man
Paulita Sedgwick as Penelope, a high-strung girl

During the above we hear the title song as follows:

> They call us savages because we dare to love;
> And say time's ravages will cloud the moon above.
> They disapprove of our untamed desire.
> How often we've been told
> That love grows cold,
> But we've invented fire.

We're called barbarians because we found romance,
They see the very answer in a lover's glance.
They'd make our paradise into a cage.
In place of rapture, we'd
Face capture. Eden's not for those their age.

In jungle fashion, our
        fates rendezvous.
We'll let our passion flower
        without taboo,
Because the joy of being savage is
Being savages with you.
The joy of being savage is
Being savages with you.

The following credits appear next:

Screenplay	George Swift Trow and
	Michael O'Donoghue
	based on an idea by James Ivory
Editing	Kent McKinney
	assisté de Mary Brown
Sound	Gary Alper
Photography	Walter Lassally
Art and Titles	Charles E. White III
Music	Joe Raposo
Savages sung by	Bobby Short
Associate Producer	Anthony Korner
Executive Producer	Joseph J. M. Saleh
Producer	Ismail Merchant
Director	James Ivory

THE MUD PEOPLE

The early morning sun shines through the forest treetops. The camera moves down towards thicker foliage. The Mud People hurry along a trail towards screen right. They are small, masked, excited figures, almost naked, jostling and jibbering through the underbrush to their destination, a sunny clearing. Here they form a loose circle and begin a shuffling dance. The priestess Khar-Lah-Tah dominates, in a black and white head-dress. The circle opens and closes, moving clock-wise.

TITLE: Shortly after dawn, the tribe gathers in the clearing.

The Mudwomen crouch over a pit of muck, which they spread on their bodies.

TITLE: Hstr-Lsl is uniquely suited to search for the narcotic leaf.

The Man-woman monster Hstr-Lsl makes its way slowly down the trail in search of the narcotic leaf. Joining the other members of the tribe, all go off through the woods.

TITLE: The leaf is passed from hand to hand. Inhaling its aromatic smoke is said to produce visions and temporary aphasia.

At the foot of tall bending trees, the Mud People prepare to take the narcotic leaf.

TITLE: A Mudchild distributes the leaves.

The Mud People drop their leaves onto the fire. As they take in its smoke they gently sway from side to side.

Zia, the Mud Child, approaches the camera, followed by the Mudwomen, who are half-leading, half-dragging a youth.

TITLE: Jool-Yun, consort of the priestess.

They hurry along a trail and then, as if struck by an awesome sight, they sink to the ground.

TITLE: Khar-Lah-Tah receives her consort in a final embrace.

Flanked by warriors, Khar-Lah-Tah comes forward. The Mudwomen bring Jool-Yun up to her. She lays her hands on his shoulders emphatically as if to say, "Yes, you are the one!" She turns away and the others follow her, pulling Jool-Yun along. From a distance we see Hstr-Lsl form a support for the priestess. She bends over it and it holds her up. Jool-Yun is led to her and, with something of a flourish, mounts his consort from behind. The others assist, making sure the ritual act is completed properly.

TITLE: Waiting for the command.

Jool-Yun is bound to a tree growing out of a fissure in the glacial stone. The Mud People wait for the propitious moment of sacrifice. Ahr-Chee, the warrior, raises a boulder over the victim's head. Khar-Lah-Tah raises her hands to give the signal. Suddenly, from out of the treetops, a croquet ball makes a slow arc towards the place of sacrifice. As it comes closer the façade of the House flashes on the screen three times.

TITLE: In the forest, where perfect spheres are unknown, the arrival of a croquet ball causes astonishment.

The trajectory of the ball is complete. It strikes the glacial stone, rolls to the ground and stops. Khar-Lah-Tah topples over, the sacrifice is interrupted. The Mud People cautiously approach the

fateful sphere. Ses-s-Li, more impetuous than the rest, picks it up. Where has it come from? What does it mean? Hah-Ree, the muttering tribal ancient, points in the direction of the ball's origin: West.

TITLE: Tribal elders are often distinguished by pebbles embedded in their teeth although such is not the case here.

Khar-Lah-Tah seizes the ball. It seems to possess a potency of its own. She staggers forward as if led by it. Three open doors flash one after the other. The Mud People follow their priestess on the way to these doors.

TITLE: One outcast frees another.

Jool-Yun is left behind tied to the tree. E-Muh-Li frees him by biting through the twisted vines that bind him.

The warrior Ahr-Chee, followed by Khar-Lah-Tah who holds her ball aloft like a lamp, advances through the dense woods. The others straggle behind, foraging, humping, peering this way and that as they go deeper into unknown territory. Their progress is observed by Asha, the Forest Girl.

TITLE: A member of another tribe, possibly a Seed Masher.

Frightened, she makes her way down a slope. A dead limb breaks alerting Ahr-Chee. He signals the others and goes in pursuit, spear raised. Asha runs, hides, runs again and is finally boxed in by fallen trees. Ahr-Chee catches up, grips her tightly, and hoists her on his back.

TITLE: Their customs appear as strange to her as they do to us.

Ahr-Chee presents his captive to the Mud People and Khar-Lah-Tah makes circular motions over her with the ball as if to

divine goodness or malevolence. Satisfied, they all move off, Ahr-Chee holding Asha by her long hair. The Limping Man looks back towards the forest from which they have just emerged.

TITLE: Between Two Worlds.

At the bottom of a great alley of beechwood trees we see an abandoned Pierce Arrow automobile. The Mud People creep towards this mysterious and splendid artifact, surround it, cautiously touch its shining surfaces. During this we hear:

VOICE OVER: Die einen sehen in allen irdischen Dingen nur einen trostlosen Kreislauf; im Leben der Völker wie im Leben der Individuen, in diesem, wie in der organischen Natur überhaupt, sehen sie ein Wachsen, Blühen, Welken und Sterben: Frühling, Sommer, Herbst und Winter! In der kleinen Chronik von Hoffnungen, Nöten, Missgeschicken, Schmerzen und Freuden, Irrtümern und Enttäu-

schungen, womit der einzelne Mensch sein Leben verbringt, in dieser Menschengeschichte sehen sie auch die Geschichte der Menschheit.

Zia, the Mud Child, is the first to enter the House; the camera, inside it, follows her through a sun porch full of chattering birds. The others approach along an overgrown columned arcade. (Here the film goes from black and white into sepia).

The Mud Child pauses at a closed door, then pushes it open. The door creaks on its hinges, cobwebs break apart, and we see an entrance hall with pictures, statues, a flight of stairs. She crosses to them and begins climbing up on all fours. The rest of the tribe now enters the House, passing through a fine panelled room. They are reunited with the Child; all climb the broad stairs in a rush on their hands and knees.

They explore the House. They discover a picture gallery. A beautiful young man, a bishop, a goddess, a young girl stare down. Peh-Nul-Ahp-Ay stays behind. She climbs onto a table in order to see the young man in the portrait better. She leans forward, studying his face. She licks the face.

Khar-Lah-Tah draws back in awe before a large bronze statue of a woman and the others drop onto the floor. Slowly she elevates the croquet ball, then places it at the statue's sandaled foot.

Jool-Yun, consort of the priestess, has made his way to the House. He enters through a window, entangling himself in a harp. The strings hum and throb at his touch. The outcast E-Muh-Li watches him from the lawn.

Later. The Mud People set up camp in the entrance hall and

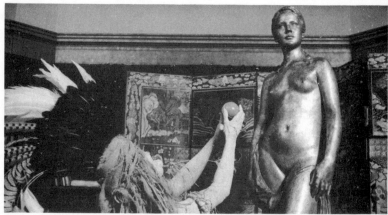

build a fire on the carpet. They squat about it examining objects they have found: a hand mirror, an ostrich egg, an escutcheon, diamonds, long white gloves. They grab, lick, hammer, croon and hump. The Forest Girl fans the fire in between cuffs from Ahr-Chee. During this we hear:

VOICE OVER: Was ist der Mensch ehe die Schönheit die freie Lust ihm entlockt und die ruhige Form das wilde Leben besänftigt? Ewig einförmig in seinen Zwecken, ewig wechselnd in seinen Urteilen, selbstsüchtig, ohne er selbst zu sein, ungebunden, ohne frei zu sein, Sklave, ohne einer Regel zu dienen.

Jool-Yun makes his way down the steps and settles himself on the edge of the tribal huddle. He looks at the others warily, but no one notices his arrival. We hear:

VOICE OVER: Umsonst lässt die Natur ihre reiche Mannigfaltigkeit an

seinen Sinnen verübergehen, er sieht in ihrer herrlichen Fülle nichts als seine Beute, in ihrer Macht und Grösse nichts als seinen Feind. Entweder er stürzt auf die Gegenstände und will sie an sich reissen in der Begierde; oder die Gegenstände dringen zerstoerend auf ihn ein, und er stösst sie von sich in der Verabscheuung. In beiden Fällen ist sein Verhältnis zur Sinnenwelt unmittelbare Berührung, und ewig von ihrem Andrang geängstigt, rastlos von dem gebieterischen Bedürfnis gequält, findet er nirgens Ruhe als in der Ermattung und nirgens Grenzen als in der erschöpften Begier.

Still later. The Mud People experiment with clothing in an overgrown bedroom: fur coats, evening dress, beads, fans, hats. Jool-Yun examines the world through gold-rimmed spectacles. We hear:

VOICE OVER: Er schmückt sich! Die freie Lust wird in die Zahl seiner Bedürfnisse aufgenommen, und das Unnötige ist bald der beste Teil seiner Freuden.

Khar-Lah-Tah enters with the croquet ball. The others offer her what they have found. A black silk top hat is held up. She strikes it with the ball. It makes a hollow sound and she strikes it again. They take turns beating out a rhythm.

Hstr-Lsl, the Man-woman monster, separates into component halves. Hstr, driven wild, takes feminine dress. Simultaneously, on a split screen we see Ses-s-Li and Ahn-Dru in the attic. She touches the reflection of her clothed form in a large mirror. She cuts Ahn-Dru's hair and beard with big snapping shears. In another attic Khar-Lah-Tah laughs inside a cyclopean calabash. She strikes her mud-mask with an ancient globe. It cracks down the middle, falls away, and she looks out, the last to be unmasked.

IN THE SCHOOLYARD

(At this point the film goes into colour). Emily, dressed in a spangled circus performer's costume, swings lazily in a trapeze suspended from a giant oak. We see green rolling lawns under trees in the mid-day sunlight and the gleaming white facade of the temple-like house. Everything looks new and fresh.

The Sanctuary. Close-up of a hand holding a large magnifying glass. The glass moves and through it we see the courtyard of an Italianate villa: little arches, pilasters, a tiled roof, gardens with tiny cypress trees.
JULIAN (off screen): You see, everything is very small. All the things are the same as the real thing, but here they're very, very small.

CECILY (off screen): Why worry about it?
JULIAN: I don't worry about it. I think about it.
    Julian dusts his hands and turns around in response to a sound. It is Carlotta, wearing a red velvet robe and gold jewellery, with feathers in her hair. She points at the golden statue of the girl and makes a growling sound far back in her throat. Cecily stands frozen. Carlotta, making a spiral motion with her outstretched arm, advances on Julian.
CARLOTTA: You!
    Julian backs away from her, moves around her, and tiptoes humorously out of the room. Cecily collects herself, rings a little bell, throws the skirt of her dress over her head, and bows low before the croquet ball, which we see is bright red and surrounded now by candles. Carlotta makes a deep obeisance.

The Library. Asha, in a maid's outfit of red dress and frilly apron and cap, moves the engine of a toy train along a length of track. Iliona, seated on a chair nearby, watches.

ASHA: The little engine is Idru—the Fire-God, and the bands of steel are Erba, his lover. They've been enchanted. Idru is condemned to travel on the body of his lover without ever finding her.

ILIONA: Don't believe her, the story is quite different.

ASHA: That *is* the story! My mother has told me many times.

ILIONA (stroking Asha's hair): Admit it, you're a cunning little liar.

ARCHIE (coming over and squatting down): Whose is it? (Indicating the engine).

ASHA: It belongs to me.

ARCHIE (taking it away from her): Who bought it for you?

ASHA: No one bought it for me.

ARCHIE (getting up): You stole it!

ASHA: No, I didn't!

ARCHIE (firmly): You stole it.

ASHA (running after him): No, I didn't. (Catching his arm) I'll give you half. I wouldn't give it to the others.

ARCHIE: You better watch out.

Cecily, Cora and Harry are sitting on a high-backed sofa. Otto Nürder is on the floor in front of them attempting to assemble sections of track. He works industriously with a sense of excited accomplishment. He is perfectly dressed, but barefoot. Archie stands obsequiously at his side holding the engine he took away from Asha. Impatient to show it to Otto, he places it on the track in front of him and moves it back and forth. Nürder boxes his ears for this.

CORA: In the city, electricity flows out of the open sockets and is attracted by the nickel, cobalt, and iron of the metal buildings which have magnetic properties. In a matter of months, the electricity builds up, turning the cities into huge magnets. The natural flow of our nervous systems electrical impulses is interrupted and, in many cases, actually destroyed. One's thinking grows muddled.

HARRY: That is why city-dwellers become crazed and commit so many murders..

On the other side of the room.

ILIONA (indicating Archie): Do you find that man attracitve?

ASHA: I *hate* him!

ILIONA: Come, come I want to show you something. (She leads Asha into a corner) See, mine are bigger than yours. (Peering down the front of her dress and indicating her breasts).

ASHA: Why?

ILIONA: I touch them all the time, it makes them bigger.

Asha has a look at Iliona's breasts.

CORA (off screen): In the country however, one's natural impulses are restored, because the buildings are made mostly of wood, as are the trees needless to say, which are *not* magnetic. Electrical leakage is scattered by the winds.

HARRY (off screen): I advise you not to carry fountain pens.

Close-ups of the trains moving around and around on their tracks, lights flashing. Otto Nürder sits in a high-backed chair puffing on a cigar. He looks satisfied. The others, led by a deferential Archie, continue to assemble track and to set up the miniature signals.

Later. Julian crosses the lawn in front of the house and comes up to Emily on her trapeze.

JULIAN: There's a strange model of a villa in the Library.

EMILY: Do you like me?

JULIAN: Yes.

He gives her trapeze a push via her big toe and leaves. He marches up the lawn where he finds Harry, Cora, and the Child sitting in a two seater lawn swing. Cora is peeling the leaves off a big cabbage. She shows them to Harry, who passes them on to the Child.

JULIAN: There's a strange model of a villa in the house, you know.

HARRY: Where?

JULIAN: In the small library—the very dark room with the statue.

HARRY: Oh, you mean, the sanctuary. Plenty of strange things in there. I never bother much about that myself. Will you join us?

JULIAN: No thank you.

Penelope, laughing and excited, runs up and seizes the cabbage, which she tosses to James, the Limping Man. They play a game of catch with it and Julian joins in. They run down the slope of the lawn throwing the cabbage back and forth.

In the arbour. Cecily and Andrew are catching bees in a big bottle. They stand in the wisteria, swiping at the bees with a butterfly net. Purple blossoms shower down on them. Cecily jumps up and down in excitement.

CECILY: Be careful!

ANDREW (showing her the bottle full of bees): There!

Later. Cecily and Andrew squat amongst the plants. Cecily holds the magnifying glass over a wooden tray on which a number of bees have been pinned. She focuses the sun's rays through the glass and the bees one by one burst into flame. She is very serious.

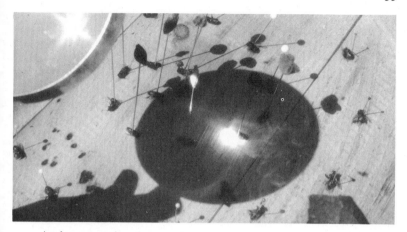

Andrew watches her work.

Penelope, James and Julian run up out of breath. They stop to see what Cecily is doing. Penelope moves closer.

PENELOPE (horrified realization dawning): What are you doing?

CECILY (explanatory, as she continues): We're burning the bees.

PENELOPE (furiously rushing in): What are you doing?

She overturns the tray of blackened bees, seizes the bottle of live bees, and runs off. The others follow.

CECILY (plaintively): We're burning the bees!

Later. Julian stands looking at the splendid Emily on her trapeze. Suddenly she jumps down and comes up to him.

EMILY: Do you want to see a trick?

She holds her two hands up with only the index fingers showing,

moves them apart, then strikes them together again making it appear by raising the middle finger that an index has jumped to the other hand. Julian is delighted. He tries to do the trick but fails, tries again and succeeds. Emily gives him an enthusiastic kiss, takes his hand, and leads him into the woods. She chooses a soft leafy place under the big trees and kneels down. Julian begins to caress her and they kiss. Soon they are lying on the ground making love.

EMILY (softly): We're making love.

Harry, Cora, and the Child are going through the forest. They are carrying little baskets. They look at Emily and Julian making love and smile fondly.

HARRY: We're gathering mushrooms!

Otto Nürder is sitting on the porch looking at a map of Africa which Archie holds in front of him. He looks up and sees James coming up the lawn. He is still barefoot.

NURDER: Here, come here! (As James comes on to the porch) I like you, good man, good fellow. I like you.

JAMES: Why?

NURDER: I like that. You know why I like you? (Rising and imitating James' limp). You walk like—like—like this.

He takes James' hands and whirls him about until he gets dizzy. There is a roll of thunder.

ARCHIE (jealous): Now, it's my turn.

Nürder drops James' hands and begins dancing with Archie. They dance off the porch and down the lawn until they are too tiny figures going around and around under the trees. James looks after them, rubbing his injured knee. Penelope dashes in and sits next to him. She touches his knee and then his face affectionately.

In the greenhouse. Hester, looking like a Boston spinster pedagogue in a broad-brimmed hat and with binoculars around her neck, is taking some of the others on a nature walk. She stops in front of a spray of white orchids.

HESTER: This is a misshapen octahedron. These are as many as you'll ever see in one place.

She leads her party into the next section of the greenhouse. They look at the plants with varying degrees of interest.

HESTER: Do not touch the flowers; if you smell them, they'll turn brown and die.

Cecily and Andrew detach themselves from the others and hide behind the plants. Cecily suppresses a giggle. They kiss each other sweetly, as if exchanging a first kiss.

Later, Iliona breaks off several orchids to make herself a bouquet. James observes this forbidden act as does Penelope, who comes up to her.

ILIONA (pushing the orchids contemptuously in Penelope's face): Here, they match your dress, they match your beauty.

PENELOPE: You shouldn't have picked them. They're so rare.

ILIONA: Rare? As rare as your beauty?

CORA (coming up): Have you picked the flowers? Evil! Evil to pick the flowers, to kill the flowers!

She gives a sharp tug on Penelope's hair by way of chastisement, takes the orchids and moves off.

CORA: Beautiful, beautiful tetragonals . . .

ILIONA: You deserved that!

She too pulls at Penelope's hair and exits.

Late afternoon. Julian lies in a hammock in front of the house playing a flute. Behind him on the lawn Archie, James, Iliona and Penelope are playing croquet. During the game it becomes overcast and we hear thunder. Archie hits his ball, which rolls close to Penelope's but just misses it.

ARCHIE (coming over to her): Now you won't catch up.

PENELOPE: But you didn't hit me, your ball missed!

ILIONA: Don't be a poor loser, don't be a silly goose.

ARCHIE (swinging out of turn and sending her ball down the lawn): Take your punishment.

PENELOPE (running up to James): He didn't hit me, he missed my ball!

ILIONA: What does it matter? Get your ball. Follow your ball, you're holding up the game. Wait! Your hair. Fix your hair. It's all over and *very* ugly.

Penelope, upset, goes after her ball. Iliona gives James a triumphant look, daring him to do something. He looks after Penelope helplessly.

The ball has landed at the bottom of the lawn. It lies near a large, white, apparently dead dog. Penelope comes up and, seeing the dog, bends over it in surprise. She circles and while she is doing this the others arrive in groups of twos and threes until everyone has gathered. They stare at the dog. The last to appear is Carlotta. The others seem to defer to her, but now she is no longer their priestess, she is their hostess. She kneels down beside the dog. She looks around the circle. No one speaks. Penelope

hands Carlotta the croquet ball, but she stops short of taking it —yet there is something in her manner to recall another place and time. Everyone stands there unable to move, disturbed, and at the same time grateful for each other's company. Suddenly they all look towards the house. It is dusk now and the lights flicker on and then off again. They look back to the white dog. But the spell is broken. Carlotta rises. They drift up the lawn, no one speaking much. The last to leave are Penelope and James.

THE DINNER PARTY

Leslie and Hester come down the stairs in evening dress. We hear a string ensemble. Leslie reads from a book he is holding:

LESLIE: "After a first introduction there is, no doubt, some difficulty in starting a conversation. The weather, the newspaper, the last accident, the little dog, the love of horses are good and unfailing resources, except that very few people have the readiness to remember this wealth of subjects at once . . . Some shy talkers have a sort of empirical way of starting a subject with a question like this: 'Do you know the meaning and derivation of the term "bric a brac"?' 'Do you believe in ghosts?' 'Is there more talent displayed in learning the violin than in playing a first-rate game of chess?' "

HESTER (tapping the book with her fan): Never laugh loudly in the street.

Sir Harry and Lady Cora make their way stiffly down the stairs.

LADY CORA: Have you seen the table?

SIR HARRY: No.

LADY CORA: Carlotta has *not* been subtle. Precedence has not been strictly observed. You have been seated on her left, and Nürder is on her right.

SIR HARRY: Well, it is inevitable that I should deal with Nürder at some point.

LADY CORA: It's very clever of her. You will not be able to have a word with him without her hearing.

SIR HARRY: You don't trust Carlotta, do you?

LADY CORA: No one trusts Carlotta. It is because everyone distrusts her equally that we all come. If she had one real loyalty, the spell would be broken . . .

> Carlotta's guests have assembled outside the dining-room. Hester comes forward to meet her as she descends the last flight of stairs.

HESTER: I must talk to Nürder. You promised to seat me next to him.

CARLOTTA: Sir Harry and Lady Cora will be more important to you, and more sympathetic to your work. Nürder has a rather less benign view on the proper place of the brown-skinned poor.

> Asha, who has been lighting the candles on the table, comes to announce that dinner is served. Everyone moves into the dining-room as the music swells up. Julian, somewhat tardy, comes down the stairs, crosses the now empty hall, bows low to Asha, and goes in. She shuts the double doors. Something is wrong with her garter. She pulls up her skirt and tugs at her stocking.

Carlotta's guests are seated as follows:

	Carlotta	
Nürder	Harry	
Iliona	Cecily	
Julian	James	
Cora	Penelope	Zia, the child
Andrew	Archie	
Hester	Emily	
	Leslie	

CARLOTTA (to Sir Harry): I want you to know Julian Branch well. He's an extraordinary talent.

SIR HARRY: One hears that our young genius is now writing a book and that it is dedicated to . . .

CARLOTTA (with false modesty): Oh, but the dedication is neither here nor there. My greatest reward is seeing his work grow day by day.

SIR HARRY: He lets you read it?

CARLOTTA: Everything! Everything!

LADY CORA (to Julian): I have heard Mr. Branch, that you frequent our music halls. Strange, I think, for a serious composer to frequent the music halls.

JULIAN: It is not strange at all. (Vivaciously): The maestro Analetti knew the art of juggling and Von Herndorff danced the mazurka with gypsies. There is much to be learned at a music hall.

CORA (shaking her head): I don't think you can learn anything at a music hall.

JULIAN: Look! Wouldn't you like to be able to do this?

He shows her the trick he learned from Emily. Lady Cora laughs.

ILIONA (plucking at Julian's sleeve and indicating Cecily across from her): Do you like that girl?

JULIAN (to Iliona): Cecily is attractive, don't you think?

ILIONA: I find her excessive.

JULIAN: What a strange word for such a modest girl.

ILIONA: I find her modesty excessive. (Pause) And I will find her liason with Nürder excessively boring.

The camera pans from Julian and Iliona to Otto Nürder, Carlotta and Sir Harry at the head of the table.

NURDER (to Carlotta and Sir Harry): What is not understood here is how very fragile his hold will prove to be. I assure you he is bluffing.

SIR HARRY: Fortunes will be lost . . .

NURDER: Yes, and other fortunes will be made . . .

LESLIE (whispering to Hester and indicating Nürder): That's the man!

HESTER: What man?

LESLIE: *Him.* Oh, I do wish it weren't impolite to point. The fat one.

HESTER: You mean Nürder . . .

LESLIE: I don't know his name, Margaret Davenport pointed him out to me the other day at the Opera. They say he killed a man in Africa, or more than one man.

    Hester looks obliquely down towards Otto. Zia, the Child, has a little table all to herself in an alcove, with flowers and candles. Asha serves her salmon. The little girl listens to her elder's conversation.

LADY CORA: (to Julian): Nürder is quite the coming man I should say. Quite the man to watch. They say the green shirts make no move without consulting . . .

JULIAN: Excuse me.

    Julian rises and leaves. The camera pans to include Andrew.

LADY CORA (to Andrew): Surely that isn't Mrs. Penning. She wouldn't show herself here, now . . .

    Emily enters smiling enigmatically. Julian has gone to greet her.

LESLIE: Here comes fun!

EMILY (as the men rise): Sorry, I'm late, loves, but I got stuck in a cab, and I can't say it was a hansom cab either. M' God Nürder's here! How d'ya do, Otto?

    Julian holds her chair for her.

NURDER: Better, Emily, better.

EMILY: I hear you bought up the place and sold it again. Good for you, Otto. And Harry. *Sir* Harry isn't it now? And *Lady* Cora. (This with mock respect). Hat's off to you, Carlotta, it's Old Home Week.

LADY CORA: Home? Things are rather different at home.

NURDER (to Carlotta, as Julian returns to his place): Your young musician seems to know Mrs. Penning.

ILIONA (to Julian): Who is she? Why does her face move so violently?
JULIAN: That's rather a famous lady. Rather a famous face.
JAMES: She has been close to Nürder I think, and to people more powerful than Nürder. But that was some years ago.
CECILY: Ancient history! Everyone always talks about ancient history.
NURDER (to Cecily): You are so young. You must excuse me, my dear. I've quite forgotten how to speak to the young. You must tell me, my dear, what we will talk about.

During this, Andrew glowers.

NURDER: Do you think you would be at home in a political discussion? I am told that I am most myself in political discussions.
CECILY: Oh please, not *politics*. (Charmingly, making bright conversation) Quite nice men turn into beasts when they become political,

don't you think? I am quite sure that the world of politics must be a jungle . . .

NURDER (now serious): Do not call the forest that shelters you a jungle . . .

JAMES: An Ashanti proverb.

NURDER (interested): Eh?

JAMES: An Ashanti proverb. You have quoted an Ashanti saying.

NURDER: You know Africa?

JAMES: I was there, yes.

CORA: Where were you?

EMILY: Did you run into him, Otto?

CORA (to James, intently): Who were you with?

JAMES: I was among the Kurelu at the end although I began in a more official way.

HESTER: I know them. The Mud People. Sutville-Boroughs says they are the most interesting folk on the continent.

JAMES: Yes, and even Sutville-Boroughs knew only the surface of the strangeness. There were traces in their society of a very ancient matri-lineal culture.

HESTER: And their queen takes a new consort every year, and the old one . . .

Hester makes a throat-slitting gesture.

JAMES: His throat was not slit, actually. His head was completely crushed with a great stone.

Julian listens closely to this.

CECILY: That's horrible!

JAMES: Yes I suppose it was.

CECILY: But someone should put a stop to it.

JAMES: Oh! Someone has put a stop to it. Someone has put a stop

to all of it. (Looking at Sir Harry).

SIR HARRY: It was inevitable really, couldn't be helped.

JAMES: Was *annihilation* inevitable, Sir Harry?

The camera pans to Sir Harry.

SIR HARRY: In this case, yes . . .

NURDER (expansively): It was the railroad, my dear boy. Don't you ever look at a map? Don't you see it was the railroad?

Asha comes into the room with a little silver tray and presents it to Archie. There is an envelope on it. He opens it and reads the message, then excuses himself and goes out with Asha. The Child watches their exit with something of a cynical expression. Asha, followed by Archie, walks quickly down a corridor into a side parlour. He grabs her ass, holding her tightly and tries to kiss her. But she pushes him away.

ASHA: Dar-ling, you are going to wrinkle me up.

ARCHIE: Your note says you wanted to be wrinkled.

ASHA: I wrote that note because you looked so gorgeous and I wanted you right away. I was lonely and bored. But now I'm not lonely or bored any more. You can go back to the table.

ARCHIE (grabbing her again): You little bitch.

ASHA: I'm not a bitch darling. I'm a birdwoman. You love it, you gorgeous man, you.

ARCHIE (with contempt): Birdwoman! (Then quickly): Say you love me. (He twists her arm) Go ahead.

She gives a little cry of pain.

ARCHIE (applying more pressure): Go ahead, say it.

ASHA: I love you, I love you.

Satisfied, he releases her, pushes her away roughly and goes.

ASHA (under her breath): Beast!

The dining-room. After desert.

SIR HARRY (to the table generally): I think you will agree, however, that things are rather different in the north. With Vikar still very much at large . . .

ANDREW (excited): A man can still breath in the north. There are people to work with Vikar, even *here* there are people to work with Vikar . . .

NURDER: I cannot see the young man who is speaking. I said I cannot see him. *Stand up* young man so I can see you.

CARLOTTA: Otto, *please*.

ANDREW: I will stand up.

NURDER: Yes, young man, there are people to work with Vikar. Even here there are people to work with Vikar. Stupid, weak young men. Stupid weak young men *here*, stupid weak young men *there*.

(Pausing significantly) Vikar has been arrested.

ANDREW: You're lying.

NURDER: Lying? I never lie. I cheat every so often, but I never lie. Check it, my dear young puppy. Vikar hasn't been a factor for weeks . . .

SIR HARRY: Never really a factor . . .

EMILY: Didn't you say . . .

A hush falls on the room. No one seems able to speak. They exchange nervous looks. A sound is heard—the wind in the trees? Rattles? Thunder . . . Asha peers at her betters through a chink in the screen. The silence at the table deepens; an oppressive fear seizes the company. They draw together.

In the sanctuary, the red croquet ball crosses the polished floor. It moves through the rooms of the house one by one, down the

stairs, and past the banquet table out into the night. As the thunder of its rolling grows faint Carlotta seeks to restore the conviviality of her party by throwing out a conversational opener. The dinner music begins again.

CARLOTTA: Do you know, Lady Cora, the meaning and the derivation of the term "Bric-a-brac?"

LADY CORA (after a very long pause): Yes, as a matter of fact I do. (To James): What a damn stupid question.

CARLOTTA (recovering instantly): Is there anything here in the house, Julian, that might inspire an artist? That might inspire a composer to write a new piece?

JULIAN (deliberately): There is a very strange model of a villa in the library.

He looks towards Penelope.

PENELOPE: The villa is called Miramar. It's of Tuscan design, but it was erected in Greece, by the sea. It belonged to the painter Andrew Chatfield. The house and the sea were his inspiration . . . (The camera trucks forward) He used to moor a small boat out beyond the breakers and, each night, he would sit in the boat, memorizing the positions of the stars, the shadows of the moon, the reflections, the phosphorous, the luminous jellyfish that hovered beneath the waves. And then, when he felt secure in every detail, he'd swim to shore and paint all night. His wife, I forgot her name, died of tuberculosis. She's buried near the arbor. She'd never been happy in Greece. The soil was too sandy to breed roses. (James and Julian listen attentively, moved by what Penelope says). In any case, a critic, a neo-classicist who despised Chatfield, spread the rumour that on the night his wife died, Chatfield set up his easel in her sickroom, trying to capture the precise shade of red splattered on the pillows. Chatfield couldn't sell a thing after that and he was forced to give up Miramar. He died in London about a year later. The villa was bought by a West Indian woman who headed some curious cult. I think they worshipped lungfish.

ILIONA: The way I heard it, Chatfield died before construction of the villa even began. That shabby model in the library was as far as it ever got.

ARCHIE: His wife outlived him, I recall.

ILIONA: Anne? She remarried.

CARLOTTA: Well, I think we'll leave the men to their cigars.

She rises and everyone else rises too. The women leave the room. Emily, before going, comes down to Sir Harry, bends over him, and gives him a kiss on the cheek.

SIR HARRY (looking after Emily): Well, it is interesting to hear you

52

talk, Nürder. I am grateful to Carlotta for bringing us together . . .

NURDER: Carlotta's dinners have their interest, yes . . . .

LESLIE: (imitating Carlotta): Do you know, Lady Cora, the meaning and the derivation of the term "Bric-a-Brac?"

NURDER: Yes, you are known for your mimicry I think. Could you mimic me?

JAMES: Do, Leslie, do . . .

    Leslie takes a small biscuit with a hole in the middle and fits it into his eye like a monocle.

LESLIE: I cannot see the young man who is speaking. I said I cannot see him. *Stand up* young man so I can see you . . . (lower voice): Approach everything in life as though you were going to buy it.

    He pops the biscuit into his mouth.

NURDER: Bravo. Not perfect, I think, but well done. It is a strange

talent to have . . .

JAMES (lighting his cigar from one of the candles): ". . . Toward the middle of the sixth century, a woman named Cecilia attracted attention in Lisbon. She possessed the art of modulating her voice in such a way as to make it appear to issue at times from her elbow, at times from her foot, and at times from a place which it would be improper to name. She was possessed by the devil; but, as a special favour instead of being burned at the stake, she was merely banished forever to the island of St. Thomas, where she died peacefully . . ."

JULIAN: As a special favour to whom?

JAMES: What?

JULIAN: Well, as a special favour, instead of being burned at the stake, she was merely banished. As a special favour to whom?

JAMES: I don't know . . . I was merely repeating a story from de

Plancy's *Dictionary.* I have repeated the entry exactly, there is nothing more to say . . .

The women are in the library. Carlotta pours coffee and Asha takes it around.

CARLOTTA (handing Cecily her coffee): What do you think of him?

CECILY: Nürder, you mean? (pausing) Well, I thought he was shockingly rude with Andrew.

CARLOTTA: Ah well, when you run with lions, my dear, you expect to get a scratch or two. Are you up to it?

CECILY: I don't know.

ILIONA: Nürder's a very powerful man I think . . .

EMILY: Otto? Otto's a bluffer. We're none of us powerful here.

ILIONA: He is treated with respect, with fear by Sir Harry and our

hostess . . . deferred to . . .

PENELOPE: Deferred to? I suppose they have to have someone to defer to.

EMILY (meaningfully): You do know it's all going on somewhere else?

ILIONA: What?

EMILY: Everything, *everything*.

ILIONA: But I don't know anywhere else.

LADY CORA: I've had a letter from my sister. There are no vegetables on the market; the grapes are allowed to go sticky on the vines. The bees hover in clouds. The beggars will not accept the coins. I've told my sister to return.

> The men are on their way through the picture gallery to rejoin the women. Sir Harry speaks to Archie in a low, confidential voice, as one privileged to know the true status of everything.

SIR HARRY: It is not generally known here how devastating the failures of last autumn have proven to be. The fall of the coalition was an event of great symbolic, not to say religious, importance. Silt accumulated in the canal. All plans to link the Eastern and Mainland grids were suspended. The harvest was abandoned and no seed corn was set aside. Oh, the Central Bank held firm, but only because of our commitments to it. Whatever Nürder says, it is inevitable that they will default. Why even now, they are massing at the borders . . .

> In the Library, the little girl stands in front of the chimneypiece doing a recitation. The men enter softly and take seats. The adults look satisfied, assured, complacent . . . This is the good life . . . the way it should be. God's in His heaven, etc. . . .

ZIA: "I have a little shadow that goes in and out with me,
And what can be the use of him is more than I can see.
He is very, very like me from the heels up to the head;
And I see him jump before me, when I jump into my bed.

The funniest thing about him is the way he likes to grow—
Not at all like proper children, which is always very slow;
For he sometimes shoots up taller like an india-rubber ball,
And he sometimes gets so little that there's none of him at all.

He hasn't got a notion of how children ought to play

And can only make a fool of me in every sort of way.

ARCHIE: Are you involved with Nürder?

JAMES: No, not in any way.

ARCHIE: You were smart. He's washed up.

Carlotta indicates to them not to disturb the recitation.

ZIA: He stays so close beside me, he's a coward you can see;
I'd think shame to stick to nursie as that shadow sticks to me!
One morning, very early, before the sun was up,
I rose and found the shining dew . . ."

Suddenly, the radio turns itself on, its dial lighting up. There is a crackle of static and the excited voice of a commentator is heard, muted and indistinct with distance. What is being said has an important sound and everyone freezes, straining to hear. The little girl is about to continue but Hester signals her to leave off. She rises and crosses to the radio. Everyone follows her and gathers around.

RADIO: This is Felix Anderwood, reporting from the coast of Ireland. A column of smoke marks the place where, just minutes ago, the

H.M.S. Dalmatia suffered a crippling blow. The flames have reached the promenade deck now and, from my vantage point, I can see scores of passengers and crew alike attempting to subdue the blaze . . . all efforts appear to be futile . . . A second torpedo has struck the portside, tearing a huge hole . . . The Empress of Brittany and the Ara Maru responded to the distress call and are presently steaming toward us. Although it's unlikely that either will arrive in time . . . A matter of conjecture . . . now listing badly as the last remaining lifeboats are being lowered. Those left aboard are leaping from the railings . . . for any so foolhardy . . . expect the funnel to collapse at any moment! . . . have cleared the main deck . . . and as I watch this great old queen of the sea, with all her lights ablaze . . . slowly sinking beneath the waves, I am reminded . . .

Anderwood's account of the sinking ship is mixed up with the broadcast of a sports event taking place somewhere. We hear the crowds cheering the players and the sports broadcaster's excited words. Then the radio dial goes dark, the two broadcasts fade away, and all is silent. No one moves. Julian crosses to the piano. He sits and plays "Follow the Gleam". He begins to sing and the others move towards the piano and join in. Soon everyone is singing. Their faces shine with courage. They stand proud and erect.

We see the house from outside. All the windows blaze in the night. The hymn is heard. Then we see the house in another way. It is dark as a tomb. The wind blows, there is an indistinct sound of rattles and whistles. "Follow the Gleam" is faint and far off. A speck appears in the sky. It grows larger and comes to a position over the house. In flaming letters we read the Greek words:

$$\text{ὠλεσί-καρπος}$$

Later. Carlotta and Andrew are seated on a sofa in the French Room. Asha brings in a silver bowl full of peaches and sets it down in front of them. Andrew is blindfolded.

ANDREW: How does it work?

CARLOTTA: Ether waves.

CECILY: I've forgotten what it's called.

CARLOTTA: "Bletology".

ANDREW: Can you use *any* fruit?

CARLOTTA: Peaches are the most sensitive. Bananas speckle too

easily. They tend to attract stray particles. For the novice, I usually recommend pears because of the pronounced stems.

LADY CORA (as Andrew tries to choose a peach): And what part do the stems play?

CARLOTTA: The stems indicate the quadrants. Fruit grows toward the afternoon sun, the west. The stems bend toward the east. From the stem, one can determine the four directions. Each direction corresponds to a season. One must simply identify the configurations, place them in their quadrant . . .

ANDREW: (selecting a peach, which he gives to her): What causes the shapes?

CARLOTTA: The specter on the fruit is merely the shadow thrown by events in the future.

CARLOTTA (scrutinising the peach): The blemish occurs in late

summer. South, south west.

ANDREW: What do you see?

NURDER: What do you see?

CARLOTTA: Duplicity, bale, remorse, glandular imbalance, obscurity, ziggurats, an illegible missive, a soiled kimono, explosions at the mill, laughter behind one's back, misinterment, fly paper, rubber sheets . . . rubber sheets, trench warfare, tunnel vision, abasement, laudanum, pitchblende, worthless endearments, trick cigars, ink irradicator, ant farms, (Cecily bursts out laughing), signals through the flames, webbed fingers, travail, weevils in the tea, trouble down the line, things best forgotten, a punctured thumb, cheap emotions, faded carpets . . .

When she can see no more she hands the peach back to Andrew and rises. Everyone laughs with relief.

ASHA (coming up to Carlotta): In my country, we use chiku, guava, mango, ramphal.

CARLOTTA (coldly): Tropical fruits are a bit coarse, I find. The decay lacks definition. The stems are too obvious. Serve the champagne.

Asha smiles a bleak little smile and turns away.

The Library. The little girl excitedly puts a record on the phonograph and winds it up. Asha stands by the large double doors with a tray of champagne glasses. Carlotta dispenses the champagne to everyone as he enters. All her guests are very gay. The party has been going on somewhere else in the house. Only Julian seems out of it. The music of "Steppin' on the Spaniel" is heard. When everyone is seated Leslie appears. He is dressed in a white tail coat, and a white top hat. He carries a white cane. Leslie mimics the words of the song, dancing up and down the room. The others look appreciative.

LESLIE: We don't need no blackbirds to bye-bye!
Or hooty owls to ask us "Who?" or "Why?"
Wallabies and sheep need not apply!
All we want are sleeping dogs that lie!

Forgive us all you A.S.P.C.A.'s . . .
We're going through a most distressing phase!
Now borzois, boxers, even Old Dog Trays
Are victims of our very latest craze!

We're . . .
Steppin' on the spaniel
Fallin' off a log.
Syncopate it, and ya'll
Be puttin' on the dog!
No difference if it's a pedigreed or a mutt, I know
It doesn't matter when you're doin' that strut, hi ho!
Steppin' on the spaniel
It's on the up and up.
Syncopate it and ya'll
Be pouncin' on the pup!
So close your eyes and give those guys a big smooch right now
As you're jumpin' up and down and steppin' on the pooch,
bow wow!
Oh, we're steppin' on the spaniel
Fallin' off a log.
Syncopate it, and ya'll
Be puttin' on the dog.

Daschounds, setters, know their betters, and must submit
Every rover has come over, to get with it!
>Steppin' on the spaniel
>Isn't it a lark.
>Syncopate it, and ya'll
>Be barkin' after dark.

So close your eyes and give those guys a big smooch right now
As you're jumpin' up and down and steppin' on the pooch,
>bow wow!

Cecily joins Leslie and they dance the Spaniel together. Then it becomes a group dance as everyone except Julian joins them. Leslie pulls Nürder across the floor on the end of his cane and they all end rather drunkenly in a circle. The music stops and everyone falls down exhausted, dizzy and laughing.

EMILY: No! Don't stop. I want more dancing. Does no one understand? I want to dance!

JULIAN (to Emily): I'd like to show you a trick I learned in a music hall.

She smiles and Julian begins to sing.

JULIAN: We're all out for good old number one
>Number one you're the only one for me
>Breakfast, lunch, dinner-time, tea,
>You feed you, while I'll be feeding me . . .

Sir Harry and Carlotta exchange a look.

SIR HARRY: Is it possible that the talent of our friend Julian has been over-rated?

Emily turns away, bored. Iliona pointedly yawns.

JULIAN: And if I have my say we shall underplay, equalité,
>fraternité—it's so old hat and très passé,

> I think we'll bring back the privilege,
> I think we'll bring back the fun . . .

CARLOTTA: Now, he seems somehow . . .

SIR HARRY: Facile?

CARLOTTA: Praise came too soon . . .

SIR HARRY: Re-evaluation is inevitable.

CARLOTTA: Dried up. He's one of my failures, I'm afraid.

JULIAN: But first we'll give a little cheer—
> I think I lost her right down here—
> And then we'll give a little cheer—
> For good old number one!

Julian leaves the group, bowing and waving as he goes. Penelope looks after him sadly.

TITLE: All the masks are off.

Archie is taunting a very drunken Otto. He raises the glass out of Nürder's reach.

ARCHIE: Have some champagne, Otto?

NURDER: Yes, damn it, yes.

ARCHIE: *Do* have some champagne, Otto.

NURDER (reaches for it): Damn you . . .

ARCHIE: But you ain't paid for the last bottle, Otto. Now, it's only fair you—you said you'd pay for the last bottle . . .

NURDER: And I will, damn you, I will pay . . .

ARCHIE: But how *can* you Otto? Where is the money? Where *is* the money Otto?

Nürder topples over onto the floor. James comes over, takes the glass and gives it to him.

JAMES (to Archie): That was unnecessary. Everything you do is stupid and unnecessary.

ARCHIE: Who is to say what is unnecessary James? Do the *weak* decide what is necessary? You have to be in shape to know what is *necessary*. James, are you in shape? Are you in shape to decide?

During this he has begun sparring with him, punching him in the chest and on the chin. James does nothing to defend himself. Emily crosses the room slowly, langorously and goes up to Archie. As she does we hear:

VOICE OVER: Wachsen, Blühen, Welken und Sterben:
         Frühling, Sommer, Herbst und Winter.

EMILY (toasting him): You are truly a beast.

ARCHIE: I always speak well of you, Mrs. Penning. (He drinks).

Julian climbs the narrow stairs to the Widow's Walk at the top of the house and locks a sliding door after him. He takes up his cello and begins to tune it.

In the Library the party is beginning to break up. People drift off in pairs. Nürder and James remain seated on the sofa together. We hear:

VOICE OVER: In seinen Taten malt sich der Mensch, und welche Gestalt ist es, die sich in dem Drama der jetzigen Zeit abbildet!!! Hier Verwilderung, dort Erschlaffung: die zwei Aussersten des menschlichen Verfalls, und beide in einem Zeitraum vereinigt!

Otto puts his face up close to James.

NURDER: Listen to me, I beg of you. I can tell you things . . . There are things you should know . . . There are *secrets*. Listen to me,

listen to me, I beg of you.

James doesn't want to hear any of this. Otto takes his hand, falls on his knees, and kisses it.

Andrew and Iliona are making love under the cellar steps. A noise from above interrupts them. It is Emily and Archie. She leads him down with a lighted candle. They pause for a moment in the door to the coal bin. He grabs her from behind and blows out the candle and they move out of sight. Andrew begins again with Iliona.

TITLE: Perfecting his technique.

The little girl knocks insistently on the door of Julian's room. We hear his cello music, but he does not open the door or stop.

After knocking several times, the child leaves.

The party has got its second wind around the swimming pool. Some swim, some cavort about the pool, some sit at tables. Penelope and James walk towards the camera which trucks with them as they talk.

JAMES: The taxi is parked beneath the porte cochere, meter off. The driver has gone.

PENELOPE: Perhaps he's asleep in the front seat—

JAMES: I can't be sure. I wait until the rain stops and then walk down to the lake. A number of sedans are parked beneath the water.

PENELOPE: Most of them have out-of-state plates, and the upholstery has been slashed.

JAMES: There is a cream-coloured vehicle . . . (both, then laughing)

66

I don't know the make. The rear window shades have been pulled down.
PENELOPE: It's possible to determine the flow of the currents in the lake by observing the fringes of the window shades.
JAMES: The wires are down.
PENELOPE: And the knitting mill? Or *mills*, rather.
JAMES: I . . .

> They look at each other, then turn back towards the pool where Sir Harry is speaking confidentially to Lady Cora.

SIR HARRY: There are further reports. The situation is beyond control. Even if we intervene, the regime will collapse within the week.
LADY CORA: Who cares? You are so *dull*. I've always thought you were extraordinarily dull. I want you to know that I find you extra-

ordinarily dull.
SIR HARRY (imitating her): "I've always thought you were extraordinarily dull. I want you to know that I find you extraordinarily dull."

> She gets up from the table and slaps the top of his bald head. As she leaves, Leslie runs after her.

LESLIE: Hello lady. Pretty lady, hello. See my titties? See my little titty-tips . . .

> As Lady Cora passes the camera a body hurtles into the pool— a man in evening clothes—making a big splash. Emily gets up to see what's happening and looks into the pool. Then she turns away.

EMILY (to Cecily): You will join us later?
CECILY: Of course.

Penelope walks along the edge of the pool. She is rigid and unspeaking. She stares into the water.

Cecily and Andrew are walking together by the pool.

CECILY: I'm bored. I'm not having a good time.

ANDREW: Why not?

CECILY: Well, I'm with you for one thing, and I'm tired of being with you. I'm going inside now. Will you please do me the favour of staying out here?

As she leaves him, once again the dark figure, as if thrown by a powerful force, spins across the range of the camera and into the pool. This time Carlotta goes over. She looks alarmed. It is James floating in the pool, face up. She opens her mouth as if to say something or perhaps call for help, then merely brushes off the water that has just splashed on her dress. She returns

to Hester. Leslie dashes up to them.

LESLIE (to Hester): Ha, ha, ha, you're ugly and your Mommy dresses you funny. Ugly, ugly, ugly . . .

Penelope again paces the edge of the swimming pool, looking into its depths. As she does, we hear:

VOICE OVER: Mitten im Schosse der raffiniertesten Geselligkeit hat der Egoismus sein System gegründet, und ohne ein geselliges Herz mit heraus zu bringen, erfahren wir alle Ansteckungen und alle Drangsale der Gesellschaft.

Emily and Nurder are sitting at a table.

NURDER: Will you help me?

EMILY (touching his face affectionately and getting up): No.

He looks after her, hope gone. As she passes Carlotta she puts her finger to her lips as if signalling for silence. Once more

James spins into the water and once more Carlotta brushes her dress dry. For the third time Penelope—now in almost a catatonic state—stalks along the edge of the pool. Suddenly she kneels down and scoops water up in her hands to wash her face. After she rises again Iliona comes up to her.

ILIONA: Ding, dong, dell, Pussy's in the well.

She exits, leaving Penelope alone. Through all this a jazz band has been playing.

From below we see Julian's tower. It is brightly lit. He is playing the cello.

TITLE: Ex Oriente Lux
The little girl, looking a good deal older, carries a tray into an

EX ORIENTE LUX!

oriental room where some of the others are sitting on the floor in exotic robes. She sets the tray down in front of Asha who is presiding and who chants softly . . .

ASHA: *Aum nam om bhagavati narayana . . .*
Aum nam om bhagavati narayana . . .

ILIONA: They were exactly the same. Exactly.

SIR HARRY: Among countless possibilities, such coincidences were bound to occur.

Zia is cutting some leaves with little scissors which she arranges on the tray.

LADY CORA (to Leslie and Archie): The first purple dye was made from thousands of snails. Only kings could afford it. It is for that reason that purple became the colour of royalty.

ARCHIE: How expensive could a few thousand snails be?

ASHA: All is ready, please. Come everybody! It is set.

Asha hands a bit of the leaf to each person there: Sir Harry, Lady Cora, Iliona, Archie, Leslie, Zia. They take it, place it in the palm of one hand and with the thumb of the other mash it with five quick jabs: three clockwise, two counterclockwise. They then put the crushed leaf into their mouths. Iliona licks her fingers one by one.

ASHA: In the centre of our capital there stands a carved temple of ivory, gold and silver. It is five-hundred feet high. No white man has ever been inside it.

ARCHIE: I went inside once. I did myself up like a wog and I went inside. There's a big statue of a monkey.

ASHA: You are not a man. You are a pig. The temple remains undefiled. (She begins to chant again): *Aum nam om bhagavati narayana . . .*

Leslie bursts out laughing uncontrollably . . .

Andrew swims laps back and forth over the body of James which has come to rest on the bottom of the pool. We hear:

VOICE OVER: So sieht man den Geist der Zeit zwischen Verkehrtheit und Rohigkeit, zwischen Unnatur und blosser Natur, zwischen Superstition und moralischem Unglauben schwanken, und es ist bloss das Gleichgewicht des Schlimmen, was ihm zuweilen noch Grenzen setzt!

Penelope runs up the stairs to the door of Julian's tower and knocks. We hear music, which only stops after her first sentence.

PENELOPE: Julian. The body of our friend is floating in the pool. He's drowned. (Julian hears this with some emotion, then draws his bow across the strings of his instrument. The music drowns out

Penelope's tale of James' death so only parts of the following can be heard). Nothing was done . . . You're not going to talk to me. He never learned to swim . . . The weight of the water . . . pressing down . . . tore away at the sides of the pool and before we . . . could . . . the swamp sucked out the contents of the pool . . . (Silence) . . . There was nothing we could have done. It was the pool. (Julian's music begins again) I do want you to talk to me. Talk to me!

The music continues; Penelope rushes down the stairs.

Andrew is diving down and stripping James' body of jewellery, coins, etc. When he has found and removed something, he surfaces and takes it to where he has carefully layed out the other recovered articles. He arranges the gold coins in rows according to denominations. The jazz band still plays.

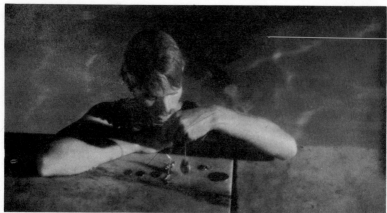

TITLE: Mating in captivity.

The Cellar. Carlotta and Nürder, with the others behind them, pause at the top of the cellar steps. In the manner of a hostess congratulating another on the discovery of some amusing new night club, Carlotta gushes her appreciation. They go down and form a circle in front of the furnace, with Emily presiding.

CARLOTTA: Emily, what a *nifty* idea!

NURDER: Forty-three!

Sir Harry drops down on to his hands and knees and begins licking the air. The others watch. When he finishes he gets up and Carlotta hugs him appreciatively.

SIR HARRY: One eleven.

EMILY: Hester?

HESTER: Asha's next. I follow Cecily.

ASHA: Ninety!

Archie goes to the centre of the circle and begins to take position nineteen.

EMILY: She said "ninety", not "nineteen".

ASHA: "Ninety!" I said "nine-*tee!*"

Archie gets down on the floor, props himself up and kicks his feet in the air.

NURDER: I thought she said "Nineteen" too.

ASHA: (shouting): I said "Ninety!"

CARLOTTA: Why isn't Emily playing?

CECILY: Emily never plays herself; Emily prefers to observe.

CARLOTTA: I didn't think that was allowed.

CECILY: Anything's allowed—it's just a matter of how much one can get away with I suppose.

Archie returns to his place in the circle. His lip is bleeding.

ARCHIE: Number . . . Seventy-four!

Cecily hops into the centre, throwing her hands up in dismay and rolling her eyes.

HESTER: If you don't do it Ces — You have to eat the monkey . . .

Later. A game of tug-of-war is going on: Carlotta is riding on Hester's shoulders, Emily is riding on Archie's. They have made a twisted rope out of Iliona's maroon evening dress. They grunt and strain as they are pulled back and forth. A white spiral has been marked on the floor. At its centre is the jewellery which the others have tossed in as stakes. Lady Cora keeps score in the manner of a Monte Carlo croupier, Sir Harry stokes the furnace, and the others cheer on their sides.

CORA: Open with emeralds! . . . Opals on the house! . . . No limit on the ledge! . . . Edges to the house!

ILIONA: I've dropped!

ZIA: Are you in or out?

ILIONA: I've *dropped!*

While Lady Cora's attention is diverted from the stakes by the play for a moment, the child grabs the jewellery and runs into the coal bin.

SIR HARRY (going in pursuit): Keep away from that!

Zia gives the stakes to Nürder. Sir Harry and Lady Cora run in and attempt to recover them. All fall in a heap into the coal.

Later. Cecily and Archie are dancing together in the coal bin. He is nude, his body smeared with ash. Behind them Lady Cora

is massaging Nürder's scalp.

CECILY: Ah—there were walls, and you could see right through —and—it was sunny outside . . . and whenever they would walk by us, we would, we would—ah . . . we would . . . uh—"hide"? "hide"? hide—hide between those plants and . . . (laugh, stumbling). There was that dog there . . . It didn't move at all—and, uh, and we gathered all around him? And I took this—uh—uh—this big round glass thing, and I made his eye very big—but, you know—hmmm—I can't remember what I was going to say . . .

Andrew finds James' cigarette case on his body and brings it up and lays it next to the other valuables. Julian continues to play his cello in the widow's walk. There is some light in the sky as dawn approaches.

Iliona and Asha sit in the back seat of the Pierce-Arrow. They are silent. Finally Iliona speaks. As she does so, she begins to play with Asha's hair, to touch her face and lips.

ILIONA: Many women have hair on their face, Asha. There's no need to feel worried or embarrassed by it . . . You could try bleaching the hairs, or you could use a depilatory cream—provided you were not allergic to it. Both being temporary measures, you will have to keep at it . . . But, for heaven's sake, don't shave. If anything seems to make hair seem to grow thicker and faster than before, it's shaving. It doesn't matter so much on the legs; they take repeated shaving well enough, but it shows on the face.

Iliona runs the tip of her tongue down Asha's nose, which makes her giggle. She sticks it in Asha's mouth and Asha screams with laughter.

ILIONA: I use wax on my legs just before I go on holiday, but I wouldn't recommend it for the upper lip. You apply it in a melted state, let it cool and harden on the skin, then pick up one end and whip it off in a quick, clean movement. It brings all the hair off with it—and, of course, it stings a bit. I wouldn't dare apply it to my face.

Iliona is down on the floor of the car in front of Asha. She begins to remove Asha's clothing.

Iliona is now nude. She caresses Asha's body and kisses her. Asha, who up to now had not responded much, returns Iliona's embrace.

ILIONA: As for electrolysis, there are no miracle methods. I prefer "Diathermy"—a method by which a needle, inserted into a follicle, passes a short-wave current and kills the root.

Both girls are now in the front seat.

ILIONA: This can hurt in very sensitive areas such as just under the nose. I usually suggest 10-minute sessions every week for the upper lip. There's not a heavy growth in your case so treatment shouldn't be too prolonged.

Iliona turns on the car headlights waking the birds which make a loud noise. The beams of light fall on Penelope's body hanging from the limb of a tree. It turns slowly.

Andrew coming from the pool passes the car where the two girls lie asleep in each other's arms. It is almost morning.

The cellar. Later. Zia applies nail polish to Cecily's toenails. There is a sound outside on the wooden stairs. It is Asha, dressed again in her maid's uniform, bringing the remains of a turkey

on a silver platter. She puts the carcass down on the floor and snatches a piece of the meat before anyone else can get at it. She gnaws the bone hungrily as the others grab at the food. Zia tries to take a turkey leg away from Cora, who slaps her. Cora settles on a mattress amidst the ashcans and begins to pick the bone clean with her old fingers.

CORA: There's no respect. No respect!

The women make spirals with white paint on the cellar wall, round and round. They hum as they work. Nürder examines a diamond he finds in the coal, cleaning it with a filthy handkerchief. He holds it up, admiring its colour and clarity. Hester snatches it from him and the two struggle for possession of the valuable stone. But Hester is stronger and younger than Otto. She pushes him down into the coal, wresting the jewel away.

The others watch dully, waiting to see who will be the victor. Hester's enjoyment of the diamond is short. Suddenly everyone converges on her and tries to get it away. During the struggle the lights flicker off, causing a panic. The tribe climbs the cellar steps in a rush, shouting and screaming, the nimbler and stronger clambering over the older and weaker. Harry tries to pull himself up by hanging onto Cora but she pushes him away.

Julian puts down his cello and goes to look out of the window. The others are leaving the house one by one through the sun porch. Archie and Zia stop to examine the phonograph which has been left in the middle of the floor. It has run down. Archie holds a record up to his ear. Nothing. He smashes the record. Zia smashes the other records and leaves the house.

Julian watches as the tribe assembles on the lawn. They take up mallets and begin a game of croquet. But the rules have been forgotten long ago. They hit each other's balls, raise the mallets threateningly over their heads. We hear:

VOICE OVER: Die losgebundene Gesellschaft anstatt aufwärts in das organische Leben zu eilen, fällt in das Elementarreich zurück!

Asha sees her chance. While the others are at their game she makes her way slowly towards the woods, and then, after one last dash down the lawn, the strings of her white apron flying in the wind, she disappears into the trees. We hear again:

VOICE OVER: Die losgebundene Gesellschaft anstatt aufwärts in das organische Leben zu eilen, fällt in das Elementarreich zurück!

Scraps of speech are heard: "I've got mud on my . . . There! . . . Bad . . . Bad . . . Ball . . . Ball . . . Mine!" Nürder and Archie

vigorously drive in the stakes.

The sun's rays strike the topmost parts of the house. Julian comes down and joins the others. As he walks up Carlotta gestures for him to play.

CARLOTTA: Hit ball!

He takes a mallet and begins to swipe at the balls rolling about in every direction. Carlotta drives in a stake, but a moment later, Iliona, singing a mindless song, knocks it over.

ILIONA: Jungle Bungalow . . . Jungle Bungalow . . .

Nürder and Archie and Emily play with energy.

NURDER (shoeless again): You're dead on me . . . dead on me!

Hester and Leslie lie on the ground in each others arms. Carlotta comes up to Julian again.

CARLOTTA: Julian—You! —Hit ball—come on . . .

The game is gaining in speed and intensity. The lethargy of the

cellar is thrown off in a renewal of energy. Hester and Leslie, reunited, drive their ball in the direction of the forest.

LESLIE: Wicket! Wicket! Wicket!

They disappear into the trees, followed a few moments later by Andrew and Cecily. Nürder, Archie, Emily and Carlotta play furiously. Emily, her breasts free of their restraining satin, drives her ball into the woods with a great swing. Joyously she runs after it, pursued by Nürder. Iliona goes, then Archie followed by Carlotta. One of Carlotta's evening shoes has come off the foot but still hangs around her ankle. She goes into the forest after Archie. Only the child, Harry, Cora and Julian are left in front of the house.

HARRY: The situation seems . . .

CORA: Surely by tomorrow . . .

Putting his foot on his own ball, Harry sends the child's ball into the woods. Cora sends the child after it. They follow her down the lawn.

The tribe's balls are rolling through the woods. The farther they go, the more dense and impenetrable the forest becomes. Some of the balls roll in groups, some alone, some faster than others. Julian stands in the sunlight in front of the abandoned house. He holds the red ball up, pauses, drops it and swings. The ball flies out and then up in a tremendous curve. He goes after it, at first walking through a glade next to the garden through which the sun's rays slant, then picking up speed until he is running as fast as he can. The glade gives way to a wilderness into which he plunges and the screen goes black.

After the players names appear in alphabetical order, we read:

Narration	Lilly Lessing and Claus Jurgen
Song Lyrics	Michael O'Donoghue and George Swift Trow
Special Choreography for *Steppin' on the Spaniel*	Patricia Birch
Art Direction	James D. Rule and Jack Wright
Costume Design	Susan Schlossman & Joan Hanfling
Make-up	Gloria Natale
Hair Styles	Martin Downey
Production Manager	Jean-Luc Botbol
Chief Electrician	Bob Vee
Re-recording Engineer	Jack Cooley

Continuity	Janet Kern
Wardrobe	Janice Moore
Lettering and Titles	Michael Doret
Wigs	Bernice O'Reilly of La Chignon Aire

ASSISTANTS: Edward G. Robbins, Frank di Bari, Howard Goodman, Roger Moorey, Mohan Nadkarni, S. Ruth Gringrass, Jessica Saleh, Jeffrey Bolger, Robert Kenner, Rick Raphael, Dustin Smith, John Flynn, Robin Schwartz, Jeffrey Jacobs, Stephen Varble, Nathaniel Tripp, Serge Nivell, Emanuel Olivencia, Susan Middeleer, Alice Marsh.

MUSICIANS: Joe Raposo, Piano; Jim Mitchell, Guitar and Banjo; Bob Cranshaw, Bass; David Nadien, Solo Violin; Alan Shulman, Solo Cello; Danny Epstein and Ed Shaughnessy, Percussion; Walter Kane and Dan Ashworth, Woodwinds.

The film was made in black and white and colour, widescreen. The running time is one hour and forty-seven minutes.
Savages was first released in 1972 in New York.

The German quotations on pages 27 and 63 are from Heine's *Verschiedenartige Geschichtsauffassung*. The others are from Schiller's *The Esthetic Education of Man*: that starting on page 29 from the "Twenty-fourth Letter"; that on page 31 from the "Twenty-seventh Letter"; and those on pages 64, 68, 71, and 80 from the "Fifth Letter".

Georg Autenrieth's *A Homeric Dictionary* gives the following translation of ωλεσι-καρπος: "losing their fruit, of the willow which drops its fruit before ripening".

Shakespeare Wallah

Introduction
James Ivory

I thought about *Shakespeare Wallah* a long time before I came to make it—more than three years. At first it was to have been a story about a group of touring Indian actors who try unsuccessfully to bring sophisticated western theatre to mass audiences in India. But the novelist, R. Prawer Jhabvala, who eventually collaborated with me on the script, and who had written the screenplay of *The House-holder*, my first feature, thought such a story would not be true in terms of modern Indian life: the kind of upper middle-class Indian actors—mostly amateur—who would have a taste for producing Beckett, Anouilh or Tennessee Williams would be little likely to take up the life of hardship which touring provincial Indian towns would entail. Their dedication would evaporate before they set foot outside New Delhi; socially they could expect to become outcasts, *mirasi,* little better than the itinerant jugglers and musicians crossing their path. I accepted this view. Somewhat later I was given the diary that Geoffrey Kendal, the English actor, kept in 1947 when his Shakespeariana troupe was touring India at the time of Independence. This was an account of a troupe of English actors on tour in India, putting on Shakespeare's plays up, down and across the subcontinent, full of picturesque incident: flash floods, hurricanes which whirled away the scenery, and much sleeping out on deserted station platforms. Most interesting of all, it contained a view of the transfer of power from the British to the Indian authorities as seen in small local events. I showed this document to Mrs. Jhabvala, who became very excited by the possibility of combining the two story ideas—my earlier one with this—and developing a theme which would be a metaphor for the end of the British Raj. Geoffrey Kendal's Shakespeariana troupe became the basis for our Buckingham Players. He and his wife, Laura Liddell, more or less played themselves in the film, though there was not a single scene in the finished picture based on an actual episode in the diary. One or two such scenes had been included in the screenplay, but they fell away. Felicity Kendal, who was 17 when we began, in a way was playing her older sister Jennifer, who was by then married to the leading man of the film, Shashi Kapoor, an up-and-coming young star of Bombay song and dance pictures.

Making *Shakespeare Wallah* was sometimes distasteful for the older Kendals, especially in the beginning. It was too close to their own experience for comfort, yet far enough away to seem to them at times a kind of lie. The premise of the film appeared to be the negation of everything they had worked for for so long. They looked upon the Indian part of their career as a triumph, and expected the film to be an affirmation of this as well as an illustration of the (to them) wonderful life of actors on tour. But the premise of *Shakespeare Wallah* was based on the failure of the Buckingham Players. So the Kendals felt uncomfortable, were hard put sometimes even to bring out their dialogue, which seemed to give utterance to thoughts which were at variance with everything they believed. It did not help that the stuff of their lives was being used in order to create a drama symbolic of a moment in history. Most people seeing the film, however, were very much affected by their performances. Perhaps this is another example of the power of the actor when simply asked to *be*. On the other hand, no one could be farther in looks and temperament from the kind of Bombay movie heroine she played in *Shakespeare Wallah* than Madhur Jaffrey. Tiny, refined in appearance, speech and manner, as Manjula she had to personify brash, outsize vulgarity. When the Indian crew first saw her there were discreet murmurs of disappointment.

Shakespeare Wallah was shot in the hill station of Kasauli, in the Punjab; in the old Vice-regal summer capitol of Simla; in Alwar, in Rajasthan; in Lucknow; and in Bombay. We began in September, 1964, and shooting continued, interspersed with periods in the cutting room, until April, 1965. The picture was mixed in May and we left with it for the Berlin Film Festival, where it won a Silver Bear for Miss Jaffrey's performance. It was reviewed well there (though indifferently received by German audiences—in fact, it was booed) and invited to the New York and London festivals. Despite critical success everywhere and a good West End opening, following the London Film Festival, no American distributor wanted to take the film for an advance, so we opened it ourselves in Walter Reade's Baronet Theatre in New York. The Reade organization had an agreement with us to pick up the distribution rights if the film showed strength at the box-office. They exercised their option because of a favourable review in the *New York Times* and the first day's gross impressed them. The film subsequently did well — though perhaps not as well as it might have done, given its critical reception. The title of the film is thought to have put off American moviegoers and we were advised to change it. Shakespeare is supposed to be deadly and no one knew what *wallah* meant (in Hindustani it can mean a small-time operator or anyone identified closely *with* something). Later, the film did not fare at all well in India, despite its record gross in Bombay's Liberty Cinema. Though well known due to its overseas success, it was not a story the average Indian cinemagoer was much interested in following and some reviewers even found it anti-Indian: the Indian characters in the film were not *good*; a maharaja, a movie actress, and a playboy were not felt to be the best representatives of the New India. It was said that we had favoured the virtuous English players too much.

The technical details of *Shakespeare Wallah* are not complicated. Subrata Mitra's fine black and white photography was done in an Arriflex camera, with mostly Kodak Double-X stock. We wanted to make the film in colour, but did not have enough money for that. *Shakespeare Wallah* cost only about $80,000. If we *had* made the film in colour, the love scenes in the mist would have looked very strange, as some shots were done with smoke bombs given to us by the Army, which make a bright yellow smoke. About two-thirds of the original recorded sound was usable, the rest being dubbed in Bombay. When the picture was cut Ismail Merchant and I took it to Calcutta to show it to Satyajit Ray to see if he would consent to write the music. He liked the film and did the score, recording it in a studio in Calcutta in two long sessions. Unlike *The Householder* and *The Guru* screenplays, shown to him in advance, which elicited useful advice and here and there some friendly admonition, the script of *Shakespeare Wallah*, when sent to him before shooting began, drew no response. Perhaps it was because he was busy making *Kapurush-o-Mahapurush* at that time.

Shakespeare Wallah—which has always been our best friend—is the film I most changed during the shooting, until *Savages*. Because of our constant travelling around North India, it is the film during which I had most to rely on improvisation. Some of what was prepared in advance of shooting was irrelevant because of location, accident, or a tight schedule and scenes had to be scrapped, replaced or rewritten hurriedly. Sometimes the Shakespeare excerpts, the style of which was left completely to the Kendals—and quite rightly so, I feel—threatened to overwhelm me. I no longer remember why we chose one play over another, apart from thinking we should try to balance tragedies against comedies. I know Mrs. Jhabvala and I wanted *Antony and Cleopatra*, but I think the Kendals had naturally to do what they were best prepared to do and what they could perform effectively with the little cast supposed to be the Buckingham Players. Sheridan's *The Critic* was a whim of mine. I think I fancied I would like to see our actors in eighteenth century dress posturing in front of that stupendous folly called "La Martinière" in Lucknow. I don't think I'd be really happy making a film which had no such preposterous and/or atmospheric building in it. For me, one of the pleasures of being a director is that now and then I can bring a make-believe life into buildings which excite me and fuse the two together on the screen.

Credits

Sanju, a rich young Indian	Shashi Kapoor
Tony Buckingham, leader of the Buckingham Players, a troupe of actors	Geoffrey Kendal
Carla, his wife	Laura Liddell
Lizzie, their daughter	Felicity Kendal
Bobby, an old English actor with the troupe	J. D. Tytler
Sharmaji, an Indian actor	Prayag Raaj
Guptaji, another Indian actor	Pincho Kapoor
Aslam, the troupe's "juvenile lead"	Partap Sharma
Manjula, a movie actress	Madhur Jaffrey
Didiji, her mute companion	Praveen Paul
The Maharaja	Utpal Dutt
The Deputy Headmaster	Hamid Sayani
Mrs. Bowen	Jennifer Bragg
Original story and screenplay	R. Prawer Jhabvala and James Ivory
Producer	Ismail Merchant
Director	James Ivory
Music	Satyajit Ray
Photography	Subrata Mitra
Editor	Amit Bose

Black and white, widescreen
Running time: One hour and fifty-four minutes
Released 1965
A Merchant Ivory Production

An outdoor performance of Sheridan's *The Critic* is underway in front of La Martinière, a vast chateau built near Lucknow by a French soldier of fortune in the eighteenth century, now used as a boy's school. The students sit on the chateau steps, the players strut about in their white wigs in front of an ornamental body of water. Animals graze beyond, and the Indian plains lose themselves in the distance under a white sky.

TONY (PUFF): There, do you ever desire to see anybody madder than that?

ASLAM (SNEER): Never, while I live!

TONY: You observed how she mangled the metre?

MARCUS: Yes,—egad, it was the first thing made me suspect she was out of her senses!

ASLAM: And pray what becomes of her?

TONY: She is gone to throw herself into the sea, to be sure—and that brings us at once to the scene of action, and so to my catastrophe—my sea fight, I mean.

ASLAM: What, you bring that in at last?

TONY: Yes, yes—you know my play is called *The Spanish Armada,* otherwise, egad, I have no occasion for the battle at all.—Now then for my magnificence! —my battle! —my noise—and my procession—you are all ready? Is the Thames dressed?

GUPTAJI: (THAMES): Here I am, Sir.

ASLAM: But pray, who are those gentlemen in green with him?

TONY: Those?—those are his banks.

ASLAM: His banks?

TONY: Yes, one crowned with alders, and the other with a villa! —You take the allusion?—But hey! What the plague! —you have got both your banks on one side.—Here, sir, come round.—Ever while you live, Thames, go between your banks.—There, so! Now for't! —Stand aside, my dear friends! —Away, Thames!

Tony motions to the fleets to engage—students carrying pasteboard cut-outs of men-of-war. He leads them in battle, singing Rule Britannia. But suddenly a white cow runs through the players who rush in confusion this way and that and the scene dissolves to a train interior. Tony stands looking out the open door of the vestibule. Guptaji passes him and asks for a light for his cigarette and then enters one of the compartments where

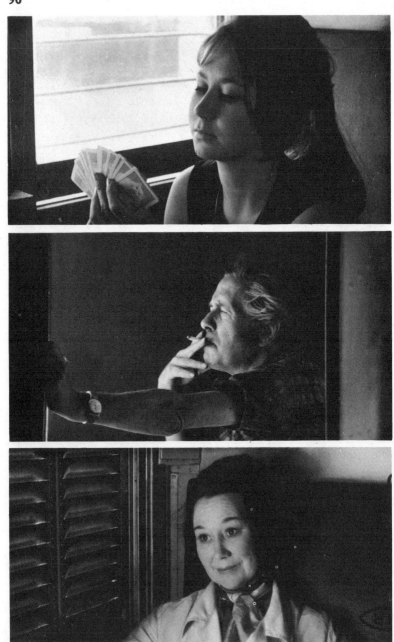

a card game is in progress between Bobby and Lizzie. Aslam is reading, and Guptaji climbs into his berth. We see Tony again in the corridor, and then he too enters his compartment where Sharmaji and Tony's wife, Carla, are sitting. Tony and Carla exchange looks. It is hot, the journey is a long one, and Tony seems preoccupied by worries. Carla nods off to sleep and Tony gazes out of the window at the desert-like landscape.

The garage of the Maharaja of Betawar. The Maharaja, in heavy goggles, is sitting in the driver's seat of a fantastic and splendid automobile, which also resembles a State Coach. His Highness is welding, and he straightens up and lights a cigar with the welding torch. Then he climbs down and opens the bonnet. An aide approaches and catches his attention.

AIDE: Your Highness, the players have arrived.

BETAWAR: Splendid. Very good. See that they're comfortable, will you?

He returns to his work.[1]

The dining-room of the Maharaja's palace. The table is splendidly set, there are candles, flowers, and silver dinner services in the Indian style—round *talis*, with many small dishes inside. The Maharaja sits in a high-backed chair at the head of the table and holds forth. The actors and a few other guests sit on each side.

MAHARAJA: Tell me, is the name Buckingham your own, or did you adopt it? The Buckingham Players! It has a most noble ring. An apt choice, if I may say so.

There is an uncomfortable silence. His Highness laughs nervously and continues:

[1] In America the first reel of Shakespeare Wallah is very different from that described in the preceding pages. Many people who first saw the film at the third New York Film Festival or at private screenings in New York were confused by *The Critic*. What was going on? Why was everyone wearing powdered wigs and what were they saying? Why that cow and why Sheridan and not Shakespeare? So, very reluctantly, I prepared a new first reel for the New York commercial run. Credits were superimposed over stills of palaces in Rajasthan much like the one the Buckingham players are on their way to in which they perform before the maharaja, and the scene in the train, somewhat shortened, became a pre-credit sequence. Dramatically perhaps this new arrangement benefited the film to some extent, being swifter and getting us into the story faster, but of course the fantasy of the La Martinière sequence was lost. The original first reel, which I prefer, still exists—to make amends we have included more stills from it here than we might otherwise have done —and its negative is used to make prints shown outside the United States and Canada. I was pleased when Twentieth Century Fox, who distributes the film in Scandinavia, Israel, and a few other countries, specified that their prints should conform to our original version.   J.I.

MAHARAJA: When I was in London for the coronation of Queen Elizabeth—of course, *that* was pure theatre, magical in every way, though if you will permit me to say it, the ceremony in Westminster Abbey was a trifle on the lengthy side, or so it seemed to me then . . . as I was standing behind a pillar.

Polite laughter. He goes on:

MAHARAJA: As I was saying, when I was in London, I used to slip away whenever I could from the round of banquets and what not to spend an enjoyable and instructive evening at the theatre . . . I hope you don't find this too hot (indicating the food).

CARLA: No, not at all.

MAHARAJA: Good. Strangely enough, strangely enough, my great love for Shakespeare was first aroused by one Miss Hamming, no— Miss Hamlyn. Do you know her?

CARLA: Actually, no . . .

MAHARAJA: A pity. She was an accomplished actress. I first saw her in Simla, playing the part of Portia. I'm reminded of her by your very charming daughter. I must have been thirteen or fourteen at the time and I was held spellbound — literally, in accordance with Aristotle's precept, purged with pity and terror.

> Here he recites with a flourish. "The quality of mercy is not strain'd," etc. His memory fails him after a few lines and he breaks off. Carla and Tony applaud lightly.

MAHARAJA: No, no, you flatter me . . . We go to Shakespeare not only for his poetry but also for his wisdom. How well he expresses all the turbulences of the heart! Who has written so profoundly on the cares of kingship? "Uneasy lies the head that wears the crown." True. Very true. You know, in the old days, in my father's time, on state occasions he used to ride through the streets on an elephant, in a silver howdah encrusted with pearls. Have you seen it, it's in the museum? The people cheered and he greeted them . . . (He folds his hands in the traditional Indian *namaaste* greeting) . . . like that, up and down the street. Have you noticed, half my palace is turned into offices? I have others, but they're dreadful places, full of spears and animal heads. I've been thinking of turning some of them into hotels for foreign tourists.

TONY: "Let us sit upon the ground and tell sad stories of the death of kings . . ."

CARLA: "How some have been deposed, some slain in war, some haunted by the ghosts they have deposed . . ."

MAHARAJA: Quite. I must say I'm looking forward to our performance. We're very privileged. I hope my choice is not an awkward one for you?

TONY: By no means. We'll do what we can with our limited resources We're used to making adjustments ourselves.

MAHARAJA: Naturally. Sooner or later all of us must come to terms with reality. We are all forced to make cuts in the text written for us by destiny.

> He laughs at his little *bon mot* and so do the others.

> Later that evening. A small private courtyard within the palace has been fixed up as a theatre. The Maharaja sits with his aides and some guests under a canopy with silver posts. Tony enters the stage area and begins to read Enobarbus' famous description of Cleopatra from a large book. (ACT II, SCENE 2):

TONY: Cleopatra? I will tell you.

> Age cannot wither her, nor custom stale
> Her infinite variety: other women cloy

100

The appetites they feed: but she makes hungry
Where most she satisfies . . .
The barge she sat in, like a burnish'd throne,
Burn'd on the water: the poop was beaten gold;
Purple the sails, and so perfumed that
The winds were love-sick with them the oars were silver,
Which to the tune of flutes kept stroke, and made
The water which they beat to follow faster,
As amorous of their strokes. For her own person,
It beggar'd all description: she did lie
In her pavilion—cloth-of-gold of tissue—on each side her
Stood pretty dimpled boys, like smiling Cupids,
With divers-colour'd fans; at the helm
A seeming mermaid steers: the silken tackle
Swell with the touches of those flower-soft hands . . .
After reading thus, he exits and the play proper begins.
PHILO (ASLAM): Nay, but this dotage of our general's
O'erflows the measure: those his goodly eyes,
That o'er the files and musters of the war
Have glow'd like plated Mars, now bend, now
turn,
The office and devotion of their view
Upon a tawny front: . . . Look, where they come:
Take but good note, and you shall see in him
The triple pillar of the world transform'd
Into a strumpet's fool: behold and see.
Antony & Cleopatra and attendants appear on a carved stone
porch above, to a fanfare from Aïda.
CLEOPATRA (CARLA): If it be love indeed, tell me how much.

ANTONY (TONY): There's beggary in the love that can be reckon'd.
CLEOPATRA: I'll set a bourn how far to be beloved.
PHILO: News my good lord, from Rome.
ANTONY: Let Rome in Tiber melt, and the wide arch
    Of the ranged empire fall! Here is my space.
    Kingdoms are clay (for such a pair as we!)

  We dissolve to an area backstage, several acts later. Sharmaji is removing a gramaphone record from a portable player. He continues putting touches to his make-up. He sits next to Guptaji, who is writing a letter. We can hear the play in the background, and faintly, coming from a distance, some singing from some other building.

SHARMAJI: Can you give me two rupees?
  There is no reaction from Guptaji.
SHARMAJI: Can you give me two bucks?
  Guptaji pulls from under his costume a matchbox, opens it, and a few coins fall out. Sharmaji looks at them, then says, in Hindustani, roughly the following:
SHARMAJI: I've seen a lot of poor men in my life, but I've never seen such a collection of them together.
  We cut to the face of the Maharaja. He's having trouble keeping awake. On stage Antony is breathing his last in the arms of Cleopatra, and as he finally dies, the Maharaja sits up and listens with appreciation to Cleopatra's lines. (ACT IV, SCENE 15):
CLEOPATRA: Noblest of men, woo't die?
    Hast thou no care of me? shall I abide
    In this dull world, which in thy absence is
    No better than a sty? O, see, my women,
    The crown o' the earth doth melt. My lord!

> O, wither'd is the garland of the war,
> The soldier's pole is fall'n: young boys and girls
> Are level now with men; the odds is gone,
> And there is nothing left remarkable
> Beneath the visiting moon.

There is applause at the end, and again we dissolve. The actors are taking a series of bows. The Maharaja gets up and presents Carla and Lizzie with little bouquets. To Tony he hands an envelope: "A very small token of my appreciation, I'm afraid." He continues to murmur politely to each of them.

The actors are on their way to an engagement in the Hills. They have rented an old car and a small van for their luggage and scenery. But the car has broken down and they are stranded

now in a desert. Lizzie and Bobby sit inside the car, Aslam sits on the running board, Guptaji lies underneath the motor attempting to repair it, and Sharmaji squats over him holding an umbrella to keep the sun off. A little way down the road a man with two performing monkeys can be seen approaching, playing his little drum to get the actors attention. He comes up to them.

SHARMAJI: Come on, Aslam, give him something.

Aslam tosses some coins. Sharmaji asks the monkey-wallah in Hindustani where he's going and what he's been up to. The monkey-wallah is quite voluble.

LIZZIE: What's he saying?

SHARMAJI: He says he's not doing too well nowadays. People don't care for his art any more.

BOBBY: Exactly our story.

The monkey wallah begins to perform for them. The monkeys turn somersaults, play little bells, run round and round. As they all watch, Tony and Carla drive up in the van. They had gone for help, and Tony brings a piece of the motor which Guptaji needs. But it turns out to be too small.

TONY: It's all they had. Otherwise they'll have to send to Ajmere for it and that'll take the whole day.

GUPTAJI: Can't help it.

It's now much later. The sun has set, night is coming on fast. They stand about helplessly. Locusts hum, in the distance jaakals cry. Then from down the road, the sound of motors, and we see headlights.

LIZZIE: Somebody's coming, we're going to be rescued!

TONY: Flag them down, Sharma.

The men stand in the road waving and shouting. Two jeeps approach, but do not slow down, and they roar past, scattering the actors to both sides.

LIZZIE: I thought we were going to be rescued!

But the jeeps stop, and we see them turn round and start back. The actors cheer and shout. The first jeep pulls up and stops by Lizzie. A young man leans out. They are armed with rifles.

SANJU: What's the matter?

LIZZIE: Our car's broken down.

Sanju orders the jeep to go up to Tony. Carla looks alarmed and warns about the guns.

SANJU: Can we be of any help?

TONY: I hope so. We're a company of actors. Shakespearian actors.

My name's Tony Buckingham, my wife Carla, my daughter Lizzie . . .
Lizzie looks at Sanju. He takes off his hat and smiles. She smiles
back, then looks down at her feet, aware she's probably appear-
ing somewhat foreward.

SANJU: I'm Sanju Rai.

The jeeps, loaded with the actors, pull up at a large white
porch. They get down and go up the stairs. Sanju begins firing
orders to his servants. We dissolve to the back lawn of the
house. Because it is so hot, beds have been brought outside
in North Indian fashion and mosquito nets have been set up
over them. The actors prepare for bed, while Sanju, in the
distance, gives further orders for morning tea. One by one they
settle down.

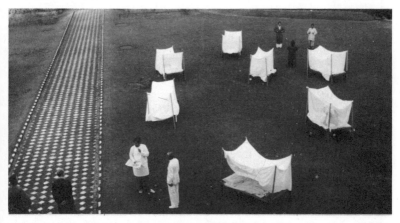

CARLA: Lizzie? Go to sleep now!
Lizzie goes under her mosquito net and begins to comb out her
hair. Aslam calls to her from his bed but she doesn't hear him.
Rather put out, he calls again, and she tells him good night.
We see Sanju on the porch. He stands looking out at the white
beds. He lights a cigarette. The night is full of sound—crickets,
jaakals, some drumming coming from somewhere.

The next morning. We are looking down on the lawn from
above. Tony and Bobby are taking a morning walk, Sanju
talks to his cook. And Carla is giving Aslam and Sharmaji
diction lessons.

CARLA: They haven't got no noses, the fallen sons of Eve.
Aslam and Sharmaji repeat this.

CARLA: Even the smell of roses is not what they supposes.

Lizzie is awake, sitting up inside her mosquito net. Sanju comes and stands beside her. He is cleaning his teeth with a *neem* stick.

SANJU: Good morning!

LIZZIE: Good morning . . .

SANJU: I hope you weren't too uncomfortable.

LIZZIE: No, it was lovely.

SANJU (teasingly): I'm sure you're used to much better than this, much better than what I can offer you.

LIZZIE (coming out from under her net): Sometimes we go to sleep on station platforms. When you're tired you don't mind. You don't hear the station bell clanging every time a train comes in. When we

don't have our bed rolls, we just lie down on the stone and cows and people and pariah dogs walk all over us. Don't you believe me? I like it here. Do you live here all the time?

SANJU: My father's house is in Delhi. This is my uncle's house. I come here for shooting.

LIZZIE: What do you shoot?

SANJU: Wild boar. I've shot four tigers. My biggest was ten and a half feet long. Three nights I waited for him, but he wouldn't come. Then one morning, early dawn and the sun risen and everything wet—the birds terribly excited, the monkeys screaming (he imitates their cries), when suddenly, there he was, in a clearing, looking round in the sunlight—and I fired, bang! bang! bang! Have you ever been on a shoot?

She shakes her head, "No."

We cut to the interior of a marble monument. Lizzie is leaning against a marble support. Sanju comes up and stands looking down at her.

SANJU: Do you like acting?

LIZZIE: Of course I like it. I mean, it's all I've ever done. Sometimes I get depressed—when no one comes and we play to an empty hall.

SANJU: Romeo, Romeo, wherefore art thou—that's all I remember.

LIZZIE: A real actress, someone like my mother—she plays for all she's worth, right up to here, every time. I'd like to be like that. When you're like that, it means you're the real thing.

SANJU: I'd like to see you act.

Lizzie smiles and then turns away and walks out. After a moment he goes after her.

We see them next by the side of the road. They've stopped the jeep. Lizzie stands next to it looking into her compact. She touches her face with her handkerchief. Sanju hands her a *pan* (betel) from inside.

SANJU: Have a *pan*.

LIZZIE: Oh, lovely.

SANJU: Don't you ever get homesick for England?

LIZZIE: Who, me? I've never been to England. I was born in India. (He looks at her appraisingly). I wonder if they've fixed our car yet. It's such a useless old rattletrap. We hired it in Delhi and we've had nothing but trouble with it.

SANJU: What can you expect from a museum piece like that?

LIZZIE: Well, somehow or other it's got to get us to Kalikhet by Wednesday . . . Do you know it? We play there every year.

SANJU: I have a friend there . . .

LIZZIE: We always stay in a sort of boarding-house called Gleneagles.
SANJU: My friend has written: Why don't you come for a visit? . . .
I think I'll go on Saturday.

> They look at each other.

SANJU: Definitely on Saturday.

> She is pleased. He has got out to close the bonnet. As he gets
> back into the jeep he tells her in a teasing way, looking at her
> with pleasure:

SANJU: You know, you don't look like an actress.
LIZZIE: Of course I do!
SANJU (after shaking his head): With our Indian actresses you can
always tell. But you look like—like a nice little English girl . . .

> With this he suddenly accelerates the jeep and drives away,
> leaving her standing in the road. She runs after him. One of her
> sandals falls off. He stops a way up the road and beckons to
> her.

> We dissolve to the signboard: GLENEAGLES. The rain is
> pouring, and we see coming up the road, in a rickshaw and with
> many porters carrying their things, the Buckingham Players.
> They turn into the gate of Gleneagles. Suddenly, the proprietress,
> Mrs. Bowen, hurries from inside. They all greet each other and
> she takes them away to their room. Sharmaji disposes of the
> luggage.

> Much later. Tony and Carla's room. Mrs. Bowen is pouring tea.
> Carla is putting away their things, Tony is taking off his wet
> shoes and socks.

MRS. BOWEN: The Weatheralls went home last October. They've

got a lovely little cottage in Surrey. And do you remember Miss Quennell—the one with red hair and such a lovely voice? Well, just after her brother Archie died she turned quite odd, wouldn't come out of her house for weeks at a time. Then one day she just got into her car and drove away without saying goodbye to anyone. Carla, I'm pouring Tony's first. And oh, I haven't told you! You remember old Mr. Buckle?

CARLA: From Snowview?

MRS. BOWEN: He died. He had a nasty fall on the Ridge last summer poor dear and never got over it. Of course, he was 87. Snowview is sold. A Punjabi family bought it up . . . Where are you playing this time? Have you got everything fixed?

TONY: We've got three performances at the club, and one at the Sanitorium, and of course there's the school. I'll have to go over there and see the Headmaster tomorrow.

MRS. BOWEN: Headmaster's away. He's always going off somewhere or other, goodness knows where. That brother of his is in charge—you know him, looks like a band leader. Doesn't know if he's coming or going if you ask me . . . You take two in yours, don't you Carla?

CARLA: Just one, thanks.

MRS. BOWEN: Did you know we had a new padre? A South Indian gentleman. Very nice, but he's got this funny accent. You can't understand a word he says.

She laughs, so do the other two. Then, with genuine pleasure:

MRS. BOWEN: It *is* lovely to have you back.

The large private school nearby. Tony and the Headmaster's brother are walking along one of the corridors talking. There is a sound of a piano lesson coming from one side.

TONY: We'd been hoping we could have at least three or four performances.

DEP. HEAD: I can't really take a decision. If you could wait 'till my brother's return.

TONY: But that won't be for another month you said.

DEP. HEAD: Yes, he's making a tour of the German secondary schools. Gymnasium, they call them. Very interesting.

TONY: Last year we had four shows . . .

DEP. HEAD: In the old days, Mr. Buckingham, you would have been welcome not for four but for seven, eight performances. Nowadays— well, there are just so many activities.

TONY: But surely Shakespeare is still in your curriculum. I mean, our shows are very popular with schools and colleges. We do a kind of package—Hamlet, some comedy, some tragedy, a bit of Twelfth Night . . .

DEP. HEAD: Where is the time, my dear fellow? Where is the *time*? Now there is the NCC of course, and our cricket. Did I tell you we took another trophy from Scindia School? Licked the pants off them. I don't want to put undue stress on our sports activities, but they do take a lot of time . . .

The turn out into the grounds. The piano lesson is quite prominent now.

DEP. HEAD: This year our Founder's Day Function was very successful.

TONY: Sorry I missed it.

DEP. HEAD: Our guest of honour was Minister of Mines and Fuels . . . You would have appreciated his speech very much.

TONY: Full of misquotations from Shakespeare?

DEP. HEAD (puzzled): No, from our ancient Sanskrit writings.

Some students pass them and salute: "Good Morning, Sirs!" Tony and the Deputy Headmaster return their greetings. The piano lesson is proceeding through a smoother passage and the Dep. Head hums the music.

DEP. HEAD: Rather nice, eh?

TONY: We'd been relying on this school. Laid our plans accordingly.

DEP. HEAD: Nobody could be sorrier than I am, old boy.

TONY: Now look here, lets have two performances at least—one Saturday night, the other Sunday afternoon.

DEP. HEAD: I tell you what I'll do. I'll have a word with our English master about it and let you know . . . You give me a tinkle.

TONY: All right. What about the performance Saturday? Plays, etc.?

DEP. HEAD: I leave that entirely up to you. Well, old boy, nice talking to you.

They shake hands and Tony goes down the steps. Half way down, the other man calls after him and Tony stops.

DEP. HEAD: But the Saturday performance is definitely fixed, eh?

TONY: Oh yes, definitely.

Tony leaves and the Deputy Headmaster comes towards the camera and into the psuedo Gothic porch of what may be his study. He is playing with a ping pong ball and he bounces it on the stone.

Carla is repairing some costumes in the sitting-room of her hotel suite. A tailor squats by her, busy with a sewing machine. Lizzie is sitting in a window day-dreaming. She is chewing her long hair.

CARLA: Why do you do that? Lizzie! Stop biting your hair. It's such an odd habit. And you must remember to wear a hat, darling. Yesterday your nose was peeling. You have a very tender skin, you know. Are you listening?

But Lizzie is not listening. Someone has come outside and is tapping on the glass. She jumps up and starts arranging her hair, for it is Sanju. He comes to the open door and looks in. He greets Carla Indian fashion, with folded hands.

SANJU: Hello. How are you?

CARLA: I'm very well, thank you.

LIZZIE: What are you doing here?

SANJU: I told you Saturday.

Lizzie and Sanju go outside and stand by the door.

LIZZIE: Listen, tomorrow's our big performance at the college here, do you want to come? Now's your chance.

SANJU: Of course I'll come.

On stage at the school. The actors are taking their bows after their performance. The students applaud loudly and in rhythm.

CARLA (to Lizzie, as they bow deeply): I don't see your young man.

LIZZIE (obviously hurt): Oh that fat thing, who cares!

A high landscape of pines, distant terraced hills, sky and clouds. A whining female voice is singing very loudly. The camera pans from the first peaceful vista to a woman standing on a path beneath, her arms outstretched. This is Manjula, a film star. She lifts herself onto one foot and then begins to dance. Darting along the path crazily, she holds her transparent veil high and it catches the wind. She embraces a tree trunk, then starts running prettily up the hill towards the summit where there are some large spiky plants. We see a group of men sitting watching while

one keeps time. All about there is the paraphernalia of a film shooting. She dances around another tree seemingly in ecstasy but then she stops. The choreographer leaps up in disgust and blows his whistle. The music stops and the dancer stands attending to her makeup. The choreographer tries to show her the step but she waves him away. The music begins again and now we see some of the other people who are watching the filming. Sharmaji and Guptaji stand at one side, and then we see that Sanju is also there, seated comfortably. The choreograper is taking the dancer through her steps. But she has had enough:

MANJULA: Pack up, finished for today!

PRODUCER: Finished?

MANJULA: You know I have to be very careful of my health.

PRODUCER: But we are behind schedule seventeen days. Yesterday

you didn't come. What is this?

MANJULA: Pack up!

She walks away, her jewellery clinking and clanking, and goes and sits next to Sanju. Shouts of "Pack Up!" are heard.

MANJULA: Oh, Sanju, I'm so tired!

Her attendant, Didiji, a deafmute, brings her a cool drink.

GUPTAJI (to Sharmaji): Say what you like, they have grand lives.

Manjula gets into a dhandi—a carrying chair peculiar to the Hills of North India. The bearers hoist it onto their shoulders and they move down the mountainside in a splendid procession. Over Manjula someone holds an umbrella. Her attendants follow carrying her make-up box, folding chair. Sanju precedes her down the mountain path. Small boys run after them.

Backstage before one of the Buckingham's performances. Lizzie

is making up before a mirror, doing her eyes carefully. After a time Sanju enters, in a black raincoat. He comes up and stands expectantly behind her.

LIZZIE (coldly): What are you doing here?

SANJU: Aren't you pleased to see me?

LIZZIE: No one is ever allowed in the dressing room when we make-up. Please go.

SHARMAJI (entering): Half an hour! (He exits).

LIZZIE: Please go. Don't let my parents catch you in here.

Sanju leans down towards her and gestures into the mirror, Indian film hero style, while putting on a matching black beret to his raincoat. Lizzie wants to laugh.

SANJU: Go on, laugh.

Lizzie laughs at last.

LIZZIE: Why didn't you come on Saturday?

SANJU: Didn't you get my note?

LIZZIE: Don't lie.

Carla sweeps in, fully made up as Gertrude, in royal gown. Lizzie goes on with her eyelashes. Carla pauses dramatically.

CARLA: Excuse me.

LIZZIE: I told him.

CARLA: An actor's dressing room is absolutely private, especially sacred to us at least one hour before the performance. I must ask you to leave.

She gives Sanju a long look, then exits grandly. Sanju pays no attention to her and leans down towards Lizzie after Carla has gone and says in a terribly sincere, feeling voice:

SANJU: You know I wanted to see you. You know that. Look at me, you think I'm lying? Do you?

He looks compellingly into her eyes and she shakes her head as if hypnotized. He smiles and touches the end of her nose with his forefinger in a playful gesture.

Backstage in the wings during the closet scene of Hamlet. (ACT III, SCENE 4). Bobby speaks from behind the arras to Gertrude. He is Polonious.

POLONIOUS: He will come straight. Look you lay home to him:
　　　　　Tell him his pranks have been too broad to bear with,
　　　　　And that your grace hath screen'd and stood between
　　　　　Much heat and him. I'll sconce me even here.
　　　　　Pray you, be round with him.

QUEEN: 　I'll warrant you.
　　　　　Fear me not: withdraw, I hear him coming.

The camera moves past Bobby, past Guptaji dressed as Claudius who is taking a puff on a cigarette, to Aslam as Laertes and finally to Lizzie as Ophelia. Lizzie peeps through a small door towards the audience. From the stage we hear:

HAMLET: Now, mother, what's the matter?

QUEEN: Hamlet, thou hast thy father much offended.

HAMLET: Mother, you have my father much offended.

QUEEN: Come, come, you answer with an idle tongue.

HAMLET: Go, go, you question with a wicked tongue.

In the audience, which is mostly made up of convalescing soldiers and a few aged English, Sanju is sitting in the first row watching intently.

QUEEN: Why, how now, Hamlet!

HAMLET: What's the matter now?

QUEEN: Have you forgot me?
HAMLET: No, by the rood, not so:
You are the queen, your husband's brother's wife:
And—would it were not so!—you are my mother.
QUEEN: Nay, then, I'll set those to you that can speak.
HAMLET: Come, come, and sit you down; you shall not budge;
You go not till I set you up a glass
Where you may see the inmost part of you.
QUEEN: What wilt thou do? thou wilt not murder me?
Help, help, ho!

Hamlet is driving his sword through the arras and into Polonious, when the scene, which we have been seeing over the heads of the entire audience during this last exchange, dissolves to Ophelia and Queen Gertrude, who has been given Laertes lines (ACT

IV, SCENE 5).
OPHELIA (singing): They bore him barefaced on the bier;
And in his grave rain'd many a tear:—
Fare you well, my dove! . . .
You must sing a-down-a-down
An you call him a-down-a.
O, how the wheel becomes it! It is the false
steward, that stole his master's daughter . . .
. . . There's rosemary, that's for remembrance;
pray, love, remember: and there is pansies,
that's for thoughts.
QUEEN (Laertes): A document in madness, thoughts and
remembrance fitted.
OPHELIA: There's fennel for you, and columbines:

there's rue for you; and here's some for me:
we may call it herb-grace o' Sundays: O, you
must wear your rue with a difference. There's a
daisy:
I would give you some violets, but they withered
all when my father died: they say he made
a good end,—
For bonny sweet Robin is all my joy.

QUEEN: Thought and affliction, passion, hell itself,
She turns to favour and to prettiness.

OPHELIA: And will he not come again?
And will he not come again?
No, no, he is dead:
Go to thy death-bed (Gone to his death-bed)
He never will come again.

His beard was as white as snow,
He is gone, he is gone,
And we cast away moan:
God ha' mercy on his soul!
And of all Christian souls, I pray God. God be
we' ye.

Sanju watches carefully. He is moved by this sad spectacle and
impressed by Lizzie's acting.

Manjula is seated in her hotel suite before a fire picking at a
number of dishes from what had once been an elaborate dinner.
Her companion, Didiji, offers her various tit-bits and urges her
to eat, but she pushes them all away in a sullen manner.

Suddenly the door opens and they look up. Manjula's gloom turns to happy smiles and expectation. It's Sanju, just come from Hamlet. He crosses to her and sits down beside her.

MANJULA: The food got colder and colder, so I ate. Have something.

SANJU: I don't want anything.

MANJULA: How unhappy I was. I thought: Will he never come? Ask Didiji.

Manjula jestures towards Didiji for confirmation, and, first from her chair, and then from the centre of the room, Didiji acts out for them in a little mime performance Manjula's sadness and desolation while she waited for Sanju to come. They are amused by this. When Didiji finishes, she goes to fetch some fruit.

MANJULA: Why are you so late?

SANJU: I went to see Hamlet.

MANJULA: Who?

SANJU: You know, the Prince of Denmark.

MANJULA: Oh yes, yes, I know, Hamlet.

SANJU: What acting. You should have seen him. All in black, with a gold chain . . . here . . . so tall, so majestic, his face in a circle of light. And what words he spoke! I wish I could remember the words. Such philosophy, such poetry. But why did he wait so long before he killed the king? That's what I don't understand. He should have done it at once. Now, if a ghost came to me and said, kill someone, you think I'd wait? At once, zaki! —zak!

MANJULA (laughing): What a hero!

SANJU: I wish a ghost would come and tell me to do something . . . something difficult, something dangerous.

MANJULA (she is massaging his neck and shoulders): A ghost will come to you and tell you: Love Manjula, be sweet and nice to her.

SANJU: *Hath*! (Hands Off!) How well he fought in the end. When he jumped into the grave and wrestled. And his fencing was very good too. His daughter was dressed all in white, with grass and flowers in her hair. How sad she looked.

MANJULA: Whose daughter?

SANJU: Mr. Buckingham's. Her name is Lizzie.

Manju looks wary.

SANJU: She is a very fine artist. For such people one can have some respect. Don't you ever get tired of your films? Always the same—singing, dancing, love, tears—

MANJULA: I have played many great dramatic roles in my time.

She adjusts her veil around her head and settles on her knees as she enacts one of her big scenes with passion. She speaks in Hindustani and the words go approximately:

MANJULA: I may be forgotten when I die, but oh, Ramesh, come to

my grave and weep just one tear, just one!

Sanju supplies the last line for her and they both burst into laughter. Didiji comes and feeds Manjula a grape and then Manjula pops a grape into Sanju's mouth too.

The post office of Kalikhet. Tony comes up the street, onto the porch, and enters the telephone booth. He takes the directory and searches for a number. We cut to the Deputy Headmaster's office. He is busy at work. The phone rings and he picks it up.

DEPUTY HEADMASTER: Ah, Mr. Buckingham. We so enjoyed the performance the other evening. Just like old times. I was speaking of it to my wife.

TONY: It's a wonderful school stage. One of the best in India. We always feel very much at home there. Hmmmm? I certainly hope

our annual tradition at the school won't be broken this year . . .

DEP. HEAD: Oh, yes . . .

TONY: I wonder if you've had a talk with the senior English master —Mr.—I'm afraid the name's escaped me at the moment . . .

DEP. HEAD: Lall, Mr. Lall.

TONY: Yes, Mr. Lall . . .

DEP. HEAD: Next year we'll surely have you with us again.

TONY: But you saw how they enjoyed it Saturday evening, You heard them . . .

DEP. HEAD: Where is the time, my dear fellow, where is the time? Well, goodbye, Mr. Buckingham, pleasure hearing from you . . .

> Tony stands inside the phone cabin, stricken with disappointment. He emerges from the post office, sad and glum. He meets Sharmaji outside, who has just been collecting his mail. He hands some letters to Tony, who stuffs them in his pocket without reading them. Slowly they walk up the hill together. After a time, and hesitantly, Sharmaji takes a letter out of his pocket.

SHARMAJI: From home.

TONY: All's well, I trust.

SHARMAJI: Oh yes, thank you Mr. Buckingham . . . My brother's wife has had another son.

TONY: Splendid.

SHARMAJI: It is her third.

TONY: Good show.

SHARMAJI: Yes, all are happy. They send you their greetings and blessings.

TONY: Thank them very much.

SHARMAJI: They remember you always in every letter . . . My youngest sister is 16 now . . . (he half pulls out the letter and then pushes it back) . . . My father writes they have found someone. A very good boy, a B.A. with a fine job earning 275 rupees a month . . .

> They stand still. Tony knows what is coming.

SHARMAJI: My father writes to ask you—to ask—I feel ashamed. I know it is very difficult for you now.

TONY: Nonsense.

SHARMAJI: They want me to send 200 rupees.

TONY: We'll do what we can.

> They walk on. Sharmaji looks happy.

SHARMAJI: At my other sister's wedding there were 174 people, best food in town, bagpipes . . .

> With his umbrella Sharmaji pretends to play a bagpipe air. We dissolve to the entrance of Gleneagles. It is raining lightly and there is a mist. Sharmaji gives Tony his umbrella and they part. Tony goes inside and takes a bottle of beer out of his cupboard.

He pours himself a glass and is just about to drink when from the other room the bulky figure of Guptaji appears hesitantly.

He comes up to Tony and Tony pours him a glass of beer too.

GUPTAJI: My elder brother is starting a business. In poultry.

TONY: How interesting.

GUPTAJI: It's a very good business. Imagine: one hen gives 50 eggs, and you eat half of them. The other half hatch into chickens and again you will get twenty hens and again they will give you 50 eggs each. 50 multiplied by 20. Imagine if you have a hundred!

TONY: Fabulous!

GUPTAJI: It is a very good business . . . Of course my brother will need some help, it is not possible for one man. He has written to me.

TONY: I see.

GUPTAJI: I hope there will be no inconvenience to you . . . What can I do, Mr. Buckingham? You tell me. Always, always they are writing to ask: Why don't you send money? What can I answer? I'm a married man, I have three little children, they must *live*. I like to be with you, I want to be with you . . .

TONY (raising his glass): Cheers.

That evening. Tony and Carla's bedroom. Carla is sewing on a ruff, Tony sits on the side of his bed.

CARLA: What? Do you want to go to sleep? Just let me finish.

TONY: I just can't get it out of my mind. We've played there year after year, four, five, six performances. They couldn't see enough of us.

CARLA: Never mind.

TONY: It's such a rejection. Of me, of everything I am, everything I've ever done.

CARLA: Don't be silly.

TONY: Nowadays . . . Why should they care?

CARLA: We've had a lot of appreciation.

TONY: It's not appreciation I'm talking about Carla, I mean, why are we here? Instead of say somewhere like Bristol or Sheffield or someplace like that. Did I have to come all the way to India because I wasn't good enough for those places? Now don't put on that pained expression Carla. No, it wasn't that. We were idealists, weren't we, you and I?

CARLA: I always followed you.

TONY: And it always turned out so well. All those people coming out from England to join us, people queueing up for our shows, the money rolling in . . . Then it all changed, slowly, over these past years. I keep thinking about it, I can't help it. We should have gone home in '47 when the others went. But we were too sure of ourselves. Indians will always love us, we thought. And they did, they did.

CARLA: They still do.

TONY: They laughed at all the jokes, cried in all the right places, the most wonderful audience in the world.

CARLA: They're still the same people.

TONY: No, Carla, they're not, and neither are we. I've grown old and sour.

> The interior of the faded English club. Sanju is playing billiards with a distinguished old Sikh gentleman in a white turban. Lizzie stands by reading the rules of the billiard room which are posted on the wall. She is bored. Sanju does not play very well. The old Sikh wins.

> The porch of Gleneagles. Mrs. Bowen is threading a curtain on a wire. An irate Indian woman, one of the lodgers, is complaining to her.

MRS. PURI: We're used to having our tea at six o'clock. As soon as we wake up.

MRS. BOWEN: Very well—

MRS. PURI: Every morning I tell him, but every morning it is the same.

MRS. BOWEN: I'll look into it Mrs. Puri.

> Carla comes up and Mrs. Puri goes into her room.

CARLA: I'm sorry if I'm interrupting.

MRS. BOWEN: Some of these people . . .

CARLA: If your busy . . .

MRS. BOWEN: Not at all.

CARLA: Would it be a terrible thing to ask, Beryl, if you could wait until next week? It's rather difficult for us just now—the school letting us down so badly. But if we can get the club for another week, then we'll be out of the woods, as they say . . .

MRS. BOWEN: It's a bit irregular . . .

CARLA: Only 'till the end of next week, I promise you Beryl. I know I can count on you, we've been friends for so long, haven't we?

> Mrs. Bowen throughout this plea of Carla's has been giving instructions in her Anglicized Hindustani to a carpenter who is planing a door. Now she leads Carla into her office and the two women sit down.

MRS. BOWEN: You're not doing too well, are you Carla?

CARLA: It's only a temporary embarrassment, because of the school. Last month we had a very successful season in Assam.

MRS. BOWEN: It's not like the old days. What do these people know about our theatre? Shakespeare and all that? John and I are thinking of going home.

CARLA: You're not selling Gleneagles?

Mrs. Bowen shrugs unhappily.

CARLA: We've stayed here every year. It was something to look forward to the whole year round.

MRS. BOWEN: It was all right in my parent's time. But nowadays people like that new hotel opposite, all cheap flash. You ought to start thinking about it too, Carla. There's no place like home. Though we always used to think *this* was our home.

CARLA: For myself, I don't mind. It's Lizzie.

The interior of the club bar. Sanju and Lizzie enter, happy together. Lizzie is carrying a poster for their performances which she takes up to the bar. She addresses the barman.

LIZZIE: Would you put this up there? It's for our show.

The barman tells her in Hindustani that she'll have to ask the club secretary. Sanju tells him to put the poster up and be quick about it. The barman does so, and salutes him. Bobby is sitting at the bar with a drink in his hand. He has been lost in his thoughts, but now he rouses himself during the above exchange and comments upon the poster:

BOBBY: "Extended by popular demand," eh.

LIZZIE: There's a funny smell in here.

BOBBY: It's the smell of decomposition.

LIZZIE: Why are you so morbid everytime we come to the hills?

BOBBY: Oh, it's sitting here by myself, drinking this wretched stuff. Here, take it away! (He signals the barman). Do you want to see something? Let me show you a mute testimonial. Do you know what a mute testimonial is?

He gets up from the bar and, followed by Sanju and Lizzie, goes out into the adjoining porch where there are a great many empty racks for bottles.

BOBBY: You know what this is? Each one of these used to hold a bottle. Those were the days when you could still get bottles. Look, the whole wall, the whole room—burgundy, madeira, champagne, the lot. You should have seen it, from top to bottom. On gala nights two or three bottles each would be nothing. Those days galas were held every blooming night. Plenty of nice English girls, with pink cheeks and silk stockings—a smashing band—the officers in their dress uniforms—take your partners for a waltz . . .

He seizes Lizzie and sweeps her onto the abandoned dance floor. Sanju follows and watches from the door. Bobby and Lizzie waltz slowly around in an old man's jerky dance. But suddenly

Bobby stops, stumbles, and gasps for breath. He staggers into a chair and Sanju hurries up to them. He and Lizzie look down at him in a concerned way.

BOBBY (after getting his breath back and looking at Lizzie): I'll be all right in a minute. It's the altitude. (He breathes with difficulty, then tells her fiercely): You shouldn't be here! There's nothing left for us here now.

The fog is rolling in over the hills, which are gradually covered with mist. Sanju and Lizzie are climbing a slope together.

SANJU: Don't you ever get tired of travelling?

LIZZIE: Sometimes I do. But if we stay too long in one place, I get fed up, bored—you know? And I think—come on, let's go!

SANJU: I'm the same. If I have to sit around the house, God, I feel I want to tear down the walls, break up the furniture. I feel as if something is burning me up—here—(he touches his chest). I want to do so many things. I have many ideas. Did you know I want to produce a film? Yes, about the history of rhythm. You know, musical rhythm and all how it started. It's ready. Some friends of mine are going to help me.

He backs off suddenly and frames the air like a director.

SANJU: Ready for take! Start camera! Yes, why do you look doubtful? I'll make it.

LIZZIE: I'm not looking doubtful.

SANJU: It will start in the beginning—with sounds of nature—you'll see an icicle in a cave in the Himalayas—slowly the drops fall— tick, tick, tick. We'll see the drops. Then the spring comes and the icicles melt and the drops begin to fall faster—tick, tick, tick, tick. Tick, tick, tick, tick. Now, all the icicles in the cave are melting,

their drops are falling at different times. And that is rhythm!

LIZZIE: Then?

SANJU: We see a river. The water from all the icicles is rushing and it reaches the sea. Now the rhythm is different. Slow, majestical. Ha—shoo—the waves beat against the shore. What do you think?

LIZZIE: Oh, I like it very much. What happens next?

SANJU: There are birds—you know, those big white birds, what do you call them, not pelicans. We call them . . .

LIZZIE: Herons?

SANJU: *Haa.* Yes, in a pool by the sea. It's dawn, it's time for them to fly away. They stand in the water and beat their wings. Flop, flop, flop, flop. Flop, flop, flop, flop, and that is rhythm.

LIZZIE: And?

SANJU: And many other things. I haven't decided exactly what to choose. It all leads to the first drum beat.

LIZZIE: The first drum beat is the heart.

> He looks at her terribly impressed. He would like to say *"Wah!"* Then Lizzie turns round and, leaning against the railing indicates a spot below.

LIZZIE: This spot is called Lady's Grave. There's an English lady buried here. It's a sad story. Her lover jilted her—

SANJU: Tsk, tsk.

LIZZIE: No, it's sad. She rode out sobbing and crying on her horse in the stormy night and she rode so hard in the dark and the rain and the wind, that the horse fell and she was killed.

> They stand looking out over the misty scene. Then they begin to walk down slowly. Lizzie picks wildflowers, Sanju lights a cigarette. The fog becomes deeper.

SANJU: I went to a boarding school in the hills. There was an English headmaster, Mr. Pinkerton. We played lots of cricket. That was all right, but the lessons—no, I didn't like them.

LIZZIE: Say something in Sanskrit.

SANJU: I've forgotten.

LIZZIE: Go on.

SANJU (conjugating): *Nayaami nayaav nayaam, nayasi nayath nayath.*
He switches into Urdu and recites a stanza:

> *Sham bhi thi dhowan dhowan*
> *Husn bhi tha udas udas*
> *Dil ko Kai khaniyan-Yad si aa ke rahegayeen*

Approximately in English this means:

> The evening was hidden in heavy mist,
> The one I loved was sad, profoundly sad,
> And memories of happier times were obscured too,
> And other loves, in this sweet sadness here.

LIZZIE: What's it mean?

SANJU: It's philosophical.

LIZZIE: Come on, tell me.

SANJU: Shakespeare is also very philosophical.

Lizzie makes a little face and shrugs. They continue down the path. Then they stop and he takes her in his arms. The mist covers them for a moment, then parts. He kisses her and then they walk on, and are hidden in the mist again.

Manjula is in her bathroom. Tenderly she dusts her feet and hums a little song. She has just finished her bath and she is looking forward to an evening with Sanju. She examines herself in the mirror and begins to move her hands in time to the music she hums, as if rehearsing. Suddenly Didiji bursts in out of breath and eager to communicate something. At first Manjula pays no attention, but then she realizes it concerns Sanju. She grasps Didiji by the arm while Didiji tries to tell her what she has seen.

MANJULA: Sanju? What about him?

Didiji touches her eyes and her lips and makes kissing movements with her mouth. Finally Manjula understands.

MANJULA: He was kissing somebody? Who? Who?

Didiji tries to describe Lizzie, but she is unable to get the idea across to Manjula, who is becoming more and more impatient, frenzied even. Suddenly she slaps Didiji hard across the face. Didiji again repeats in gestures a description of Lizzie. After a moment Manjula understands.

MANJULA: The English girl?

Didiji nods. Manjula goes and sits down on the edge of the

bathtub and begins doing her nails. After a time she beckons to Didiji, who goes to her, squatting down beside her. Her mind is working. In sign language she tells Didiji to bring Lizzie to her. Didiji nods and gestures to her, as if to say "Don't worry, leave her to me." Manjula smiles. Tenderly she touches Didiji's face where she has slapped her. Didiji grasps her hand and holds it against herself in a gesture of devotion. Manjula, deeply thoughtful, continues humming to herself.

Lizzie is balancing herself on the see-saw at Gleneagles. Aslam stands against a tree in a dramatic soulful artist pose. Didi watches the two of them from over the wall, and Manjula watches everybody from her window. Suddenly, Lizzie gets off the see-saw and tosses her hat towards Aslam.

LIZZIE: I'm going for a walk.

ASLAM: Shall I come with you?

LIZZIE: No.

ASLAM: What about your hat?

LIZZIE: Keep it for me.

She goes out the gate. Didiji comes up to her and takes her by the arm. Lizzie pulls back. Didiji points to Manjula in the window. Manjula beckons to Lizzie to come to her. Reluctantly, but too polite to say no, Lizzie lets herself be led away to Manjula. Inside Manjula's hotel, in the sunroom, she sits waiting demurely for Lizzie's arrival. When they are both settled and while Manjula has a good look, a tea cart is rolled in by Didiji. Manjula begins to pour the tea.

MANJULA: He has spoken so much about you. So much praise. Two sugar? Three?

LIZZIE: No sugar.

MANJULA: Oh? You are not a sweet person? Now I—I am a very sweet person. (She drops several lumps into her tea and gives a merry tinkle of laughter. Lizzie remains stony-faced.) We have so much to talk about. Two artists together—We have such a lot in common. You have been in film also? No? Oh, it is a pity . . . Never mind, I think stage must also be very interesting. You have many admirers? No please, no modesty. I know how it is. I have six fan clubs, every day 500 letters. Sometimes one gets so tired of admirers . . . (She touches her brow with her fingertips as if it's all too much). When I saw you, I knew at once we would be great friends, I told Didiji. And after all the praises I have heard about you from Sanjuji . . .

Lizzie looks at her suddenly, in disbelief.

MANJULA: Such a fine artist, so sweet, so simple, just like a little sister from the village . . . Oh, my head. You have known him long? I have known him for a very long time. There is no woman who has known him so long and as well as I have. And there have been many, many. He's like a child. When he sees something new: "Oh, I must have it." But he grows tired very quickly. Then he comes to me: "Manjula, I'm tired, let me be with you. And I take him, I hold him in my arms. Rest now, rest . . ."

She speaks with real tenderness. Lizzie's hand is nervously fidgeting with a dish of nuts. Manjula pushes them towards her.

MANJULA: Eat now, eat, take some.

Feeling herself hemmed in and trapped, Lizzie pushes them back roughly and they overturn on the floor. Didiji goes down on her hands and knees to start picking them up. Manjula seizes Lizzie by the arm and pulls her close to her.

MANJULA: I get very angry when others run after him, you under-

stand, very angry.

Suddenly the door opens and Sanju enters. He is horrified to see the two women together. Without a word, Lizzie breaks away and rushing past him, goes out. He follows her. At the main entrance of the hotel he catches up with her.

SANJU: Lizzie!

LIZZIE: Go back to that beauty queen of yours.

She breaks into a run and goes down the path towards Gleneagles. Sanju tries to follow her, but Aslam catches him by the arm.

ASLAM: Why are you in such a hurry today? I thought you and I could have a chat, about this and that.

Lizzie has disappeared and Sanju turns away. A madman goes by, ringing a little bell.

The next morning. The troupe is leaving. They are making their good-byes to Mrs. Bowen. She and Carla embrace and promise to write. Bearers carry their things up the path, and the actors are on their way again. Mrs. Bowen watches them from below. She and Carla wave.

A small mountain town. The Buckingham Players have stopped for refreshment. Aslam reads aloud from a newspaper about a sensational Mexican murder case. Eighty girls have been done to death in the operation of a white slave ring. Bobby is sitting in the car alone. Sharmaji offers him some hot *pakoras* but he refuses. Suddenly, with a roar and a grinding of brakes, Sanju drives up in his white Mercedes and gets out. As he comes up to them, Lizzie pointedly moves away.

TONY: Well, look who's here.

ASLAM: What a coincidence.

SANJU: Permit me to say, sir, how much I enjoyed your performance of Hamlet.

TONY: Music to our ears, sing on.

SANJU: I was so moved, such a fine grand performance.

TONY: Good of you to say so. I'd been thinking you young fellows only cared for your film stars.

SANJU: Oh, no sir. I don't care for film stars at all. It is a very interesting play.

TONY: I've always thought so . . .

SANJU: It's very symbolic.

TONY: I see you and I will have to have a discussion about it one of these days. You on your way to Simla also?

Lizzie has gone to sit in the car with Bobby. At first he doesn't notice her. He seems asleep. Sharmaji offers him a *pakora*.

LIZZIE: Bobby? Bobby, are you on a diet?

BOBBY (declining the food): Don't worry about me. Go and be with your boyfriend. He's much nicer than I am. You're a good girl, Lizzie. I've been sitting here watching you, all of you, and wondering about you. You know, when you're young, you never think, and when you're old, you're too tired to think.

Sanju comes up to them but Lizzie ignores him.

SANJU: Come in the car with me Lizzie.

She doesn't answer him or look towards him.

BOBBY: Go on, young to young and old to old, and the devil take the hindmost . . .

LIZZIE: You sure you don't want something?

He shakes his head. She gets down and goes to Sanju's car. Tony and Carla tell him to drive carefully. They get in and drive away with a roar. Aslam, who is washing his face, looks after them. The others prepare to leave.

Sanju and Lizzie are riding in Sanju's open convertible.

LIZZIE: How did you find out where we were going?

SANJU: Didn't I tell you I had my spies all over India?

LIZZIE: You didn't tell me you had your mistresses as well.

SANJU: Mistresses? Oh, you mean Manjula. She's just a cousin.

LIZZIE: Some cousin!

Sanju begins to sing a little song and is soon shouting it at the top of his lungs. Gradually Lizzie relents and begins to enjoy the ride and his company. The car drives away up the mountainside towards Simla.

Later in the afternoon. The Buckinghams are making their way slowly in their old car, followed by the van, with the other actors. Tony, Carla, and Bobby are sitting in the Ford, the same car that had broken down in the desert. It seems it will break down any minute now, as it wheezes and puffs around the steep curves.

CARLA: We'll have to send her to England, Tony. Soon. There's no future for her here, neither as an actress nor—just no future.

TONY: You seemed to do all right.

CARLA: That was quite different. Nowadays . . . No, she must go. It isn't as if she'd mind going, I know. She doesn't have the feelings about the place that we have, or the memories . . .

During these words Bobby has suddenly become very ill. He has tried to get their attention. Finally he slaps the back of the seat with his hand and then he slumps into his corner. Carla gasps, Tony puts on the brakes. The van stops and the others

climb down and rush towards the Ford. The camera moves away from this scene and the roadside dissolves to an abandoned English cemetery full of moss covered classical tombs. A funeral procession is approaching the camera. The actors carry a coffin and an Indian minister reads the burial service in an almost undecipherable, yet moving form of English. The procession dissolves to the graveside and the end of the funeral service. The Buckinghams and the minister drop earth onto the coffin.

The stagedoor of the Gaiety Theatre, Simla. A performance is in progress and Sharmaji, dressed as Feste, stands guarding the door. Suddenly there is a banging on it. Sanju wants to be let in.

SHARMAJI: Shhh—the show is on!

SANJU: Let me in!

SHARMAJI: Do you think all doors are open to you? Who are you, a filmstar?

SANJU: Who are you to keep me out?

SHARMAJI: I am Sharmaji. I say who comes in, and who stays *out!* He shuts the door, but Sanju forces it and comes in. Onstage, Twelfth Night is going on. It is the Yellow-stocking scene, ACT III, SCENE 4. Carla as Olivia, Tony as Malvolio, Lizzie as Maria.

OLIVIA: Why, how now, Malvolio!

MALVOLIO: Sweet lady, ho, ho.

OLIVIA: Smilest thou? I sent for thee upon a sad occasion.

MALVOLIO: Sad, Madam, I could be sad: this does make some obstruction in the blood, this cross-gartering; but what of that? if it please the eye of one, it is as the old proverb, "Please one, and please all."

OLIVIA: Why, how dost thou, man? what is the matter with thee?

MALVOLIO: Not black in my mind, though yellow in my legs. It did come to his hands, and commands shall be executed: I think we do know the sweet Roman hand.

OLIVIA: Wilt thou go to bed, Malvolio?

MALVOLIO: To bed! ay, sweet-heart, and I'll come to thee.

OLIVIA: Heaven's restore me! Why dost thou smile so and kiss thy hand so oft?

MALVOLIO: 'Some are born great,'—

OLIVIA: Ha!

MALVOLIO: 'some achieve greatness,'—

OLIVIA: What meanest thou by that, Malvolio?

MALVOLIO: 'And some have greatness thrust upon them.'

OLIVIA: Heaven restore thee!

MALVOLIO: Remember who commended thy yellow stockings—
OLIVIA: Thy yellow stockings!
MALVOLIO: And wished to see thee cross-gartered.
OLIVIA: Cross-gartered!
MALVOLIO: Go to, thou art made, if thou desirest to be so—
OLIVIA: Am I made?
MALVOLIO: If not, let me see thee a servant still.
OLIVIA: Why, this is very midsummer madness.
SERVANT: Madam, the young gentleman of the Count Orsino's is returned: I could hardly entreat him back: he attends your ladyship's pleasure.
OLIVIA: I'll come to him. Good Maria, let this fellow be looked to. Where's my cousin Toby? Let some of my people have a special care of him: I would not have him miscarry for the half of my dowry.

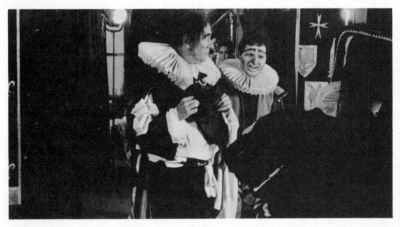

MALVOLIO: O, ho! Do you come near me now? No worse man than Sir Toby to look to me! . . . And when she went away now, 'Let this fellow be looked to' fellow! not Malvolio, nor after my degree, but fellow. . . . Well, Jove, not I, is the doer of this, and he is to be thanked. Jove, I thank thee!

Lizzie returns to the wings. She is happy to see Sanju. They stand close together. He tickles her, but she is serious and pays no attention, brushing him off. The curtain falls, there is applause.

SANJU: Aren't they good . . .
LIZZIE: Mmmmmm— grand.

He tries to clasp her around the waist, but she pulls away and joins Feste onstage for his last song: "When as I was, and a tiny little boy, with a heigh ho, the wind and the rain." She leaves Sanju standing in the wings. He looks put out.

The terrace of Sanju's hotel, overlooking the city of Simla. He's drinking a beer and listening to a cricket match on a portable radio. Didiji enters behind him and obtains his attention by clapping. He looks at her in dismay, tells her to go away. She looks crestfallen, but goes to summon Manjula, who waits outside. She comes up to him and stands a few feet away.

SANJU: What are you doing here?

MANJULA: I left the shooting. I was tired and I wanted a rest.

SANJU: You'd better go back.

MANJULA: I wanted to see you.

SANJU: How did you know I was here?

MANJULA: Found out.

A crowd of fans is gathering beyond the terrace. They stare and point.

SANJU: How? Oh sit down, don't stand there like that.

She sits, looks about, sniffs the air.

MANJULA: I think the nights must be cold here.

SANJU: Did I ever tell you that you're a very stupid and vicious woman?

She laughs, giving him a seductive smile.

The much less opulent terrace of the Buckingham's hotel, also overlooking the city. Carla is painting a backdrop for one of their plays, imitating on cloth one of the mosaics from Ravenna. Lizzie is busy burning the sides of a piece of paper in order to make an "ancient" scroll.

CARLA: One Easter your Aunt Stella and I were boating on the river in Bedford. Suddenly there was a terrible storm. We got drenched. Our brand new dresses were made of a crepe sort of stuff, and they shrank. Our Easter bonnets were covered with pink rosebuds . . . How we laughed! What a downpour. Poor dresses, poor rosebuds!

LIZZIE: Like the monsoon.

CARLA: No, no. Not at all like the monsoon. The rain is different at home . . . You know, Lizzie, your Aunt Stella, in her last letter, wrote again asking us to send you. I think it would be a good idea if you went for awhile. It's a wonderful opportunity. It's close to Stratford. You'd be able to see all the plays, and, who knows, well, why not? You might even work there.

LIZZIE: I'm all right here.

CARLA: How do you know? You've never been to England.

LIZZIE: So what.

CARLA: Your father and I used to go to a place where there was a lake, with swans on it, can you imagine? And there was an old vicarage, but there was nobody living in it. We used to slip into the

garden and pick blackberries.

LIZZIE: I want to live here.

CARLA: But you don't know what it's like. Everything is different when you belong to a place, when it's yours. Lizzie, please go . . .

LIZZIE: I can't.

CARLA: It's that boy, isn't it? You're silly. You'll meet so many nice boys in England, you'll see. And you know, Lizzie, people in our profession don't always make very good partners for people outside it . . . You wouldn't marry him?

LIZZIE: If he asked me you don't know what I wouldn't do.

She says this with finality.

The bedroom of Manjula's hotel suite. She sits in her negligee sorting out publicity photographs in a big window overlooking

the valley. Sanju is lying with his shoes off on her bed.

MANJULA: Tell me, which one for Filmfare and which one for Screen?

SANJU: Send both to each, then they can choose.

MANJULA: But what if they choose the same one? Sanju, help me decide.

SANJU: Send that one to Filmfare.

MANJULA: This? But it makes my face so big!

SANJU: Then why do you get Didiji to bribe your cameraman to give you huge close-ups if you're worried about your face being so big? That's the difference between you and a real artist like Lizzie. You should see her onstage. I wish you could.

MANJULA: I also wish, Sanjuji.

SANJU: People don't care for the theatre so much these days. Only for films.

MANJULA: Tsk, tsk. (As if struck by a sudden thought.) Please take me one day.

SANJU: Really? You'll come. That would be so wonderful for them. If you come, others will come. It will be a gala occasion.

He looks happy and excited.

MANJULA: I've selected these three finally. Do you think they're too much alike.

SANJU: Would you leave those things before I throw them out of the window—and come here . . .

On stage in the Gaiety Theatre. A performance of Othello. Desdemona (Lizzie) lies asleep in a tent-like bed. Othello (Tony) enters and stands over the bed:

OTHELLO: It is the cause, it is the cause, my soul—
    Let me not name it to you, you chaste stars! —
    It is the cause . . .

In the audience, we see Sanju sitting alone in the centre box. Suddenly the door opens and Manjula, accompanied by Didiji and the theatre manager, appears in all her glory. She enters the box like a queen, confident of her charms, and for some little time, as ostentatiously as possible, arranges herself comfortably. During this interruption the audience gradually become aware that she has come in and a buzz of excited comment is heard. It grows in volume. The people sitting upstairs crowd to look over the railing at the source of the commotion and a press photographer suddenly appears from a side aisle and flashes a flash camera. At this gross action, Tony stops the play and comes to the footlights. With his sword he strikes the stage several times.

TONY: When you're quiet we'll continue!

Manjula looks questioningly at Sanju and he puts his finger to his lips. He is ashamed, but she merely looks amused. After a moment the play continues:

OTHELLO: . . . Put out the light, and then put out the light:
    If I quench thee, thou flaming minister,
    I can again thy former light restore,
    Should I repent me: but once put out thy light,
    Thou cunning'st pattern of excelling nature,
    I know not where is that Promethean heat
    That can thy light relume. When I have pluck'd the rose,
    I cannot give it vital growth again,
    It must needs wither: I'll smell it on the tree . . .

Desdemona stirs and then sits up in bed.

OTHELLO: That handkerchief which I so loved and gave thee
    Thou gavest to Cassio.

DESDEMONA: No, by my life and soul!
　　　　　　Send for the man, and ask him.
OTHELLO: Sweet soul, take heed,
　　　　　Take heed of perjury; thou art on thy death-bed.
DESDEMONA: Ay, but not yet to die.
OTHELLO: Yes, presently:
　　　　　Therefore confess thee freely of thy sin;
　　　　　For to deny each article with oath
　　　　　Cannot remove nor choke the strong conception
　　　　　That I do groan withal. Thou art to die.
DESDEMONA: Then Lord have mercy on me!
OTHELLO: I say, amen.
DESDEMONA: And have you mercy too! I never did
　　　　　　Offend you in my life; never loved Cassio

　　　　　But with such general warranty of heaven
　　　　　As I might love; I never gave him token . . .
During this Manjula has not yet settled down. She waves to a
friend in the audience, and someone passes her up an autograph
book to sign. She asks Didiji for her *pan* and gives some to Sanju,
whooping with laughter when he accidentally bites her finger
as she shoves the *pan* into his mouth. Now Othello is about to
murder Desdemona and he throws her down onto the bed.
Desdemona pleads with him and Manjula contemptuously
measures Lizzie's talents as an actress.
OTHELLO: . . . Out, strumpet! weep'st thou for him to my face?
DESDEMONA: O, banish me, my lord, but kill me not!
OTHELLO: Down, strumpet!
DESDEMONA: Kill me tomorrow: let me live tonight!

OTHELLO: It is too late . . . (he smothers her)

. . . Not dead? not yet quite dead? I that am cruel am yet merciful; I would not have thee linger in thy pain: So, so . . .

Othello stabs Desdemona and though Manjula until now had been untouched by the play, at this she covers her eyes with her hands in horror. Othello hovers over the dead Desdemona. Knocks are heard offstage and Manjula peeps through her fingers.

OTHELLO: . . . Who's there? 'tis Emilia. By and by . . . no more moving? Still as the grave. Shall she come in? If she come in, she'll sure speak to my wife: My wife! what wife? I have no wife . . .

Manjula decides she has seen enough and turns to Sanju.

MANJULA: Sanju, let's go . . .

SANJU (dismayed): Why?

Without further ado she gets up, gathers her things, and leaves the box. Didiji and the theatre manager accompany her. She waits at the door for Sanju to come after her, but he gets up and pointedly closes the doors of the box in her face. She is startled but recovers herself enough to sign autographs, for a number of people have come out of their boxes to see her and stand in the corridor. The play continues and we hear Othello as Manjula signs, "What? Cassio not killed? then sweet revenge . . ."

Tony is in his dressing room after the play. He begins to remove his jewellery. Sanju comes and knocks at the door.

TONY: Yeah.

SANJU: I'm very sorry, sir, for what has happened. Very sorry . . .

TONY: Lets just call it the victory of the moving pictures over the theatre.

SANJU: It's bad. It should not have happened.

TONY: Oh all sorts of things happen all the time. It's not your fault—You just have to learn to put up with it, to get used to it.

SANJU: It was such wonderful acting.

TONY: Oh what the hell does it matter! If the audience gets out of hand and we can't hold them, it's our fault, not theirs. It was wrong of me to speak to them like that, unprofessional of me. People don't seem to understand what an incredible nervous strain it is to do a part like Othello.

SANJU: You were very good, all of you were very good.

TONY: I shouldn't have done what I did. I shouldn't have spoken to them like that. It was wrong of me. Years ago David Garrick did what I did and he had to go down the next night on his knees to a house of drunken nincompoops. David Garrick mind you. Do you

know who he was? The mummers lot . . .

Carla enters, nodding grimly to Sanju.

SANJU: Please let me apologize for the disturbance . . . Excuse me.
He exits and Tony begins to remove his make-up.

Manjula is in her hotel room. She sits in an armchair and is
pouring herself some coffee from a tray. She is in her nightdress
but still wearing some of her jewellery. Sanju comes in and pauses
for a moment in the doorway, and then comes towards her. He
is very angry.

SANJU: How could you do that? Making a display of yourself and
then leaving before the end.

MANJULA: It must have been very near the end, Sanjuji, he'd killed
the heroine. And what was it? How can you like something like that?
All that moaning and groaning, so bloodthirsty. And so badly acted.

SANJU: I should have known you couldn't appreciate such things.
Just tell me, why did you bring that press photographer into the
theatre like that? I think you planned it from the beginning.

MANJULA: I didn't bring him. It must have been the theatre manager.
What can I do if someone wants to take my picture, say "No, no"?

SANJU: You think you can get away with a thing like this? Do you
know how it made me feel, sitting there with you? And Mr. Buckingham, how he felt?

MANJULA: For them it is an honor if I stay even five minutes. Everything so dirty and shabby! When I came back, at once I told Didiji
to make my bath ready. The chair they gave me was broken, I'm
sure it had bugs. *Chi!*

SANJU: Oh, stupid, stupid . . .

MANJULA: Yes, I'm stupid and they're very clever, with their dirty

costumes in that cheap hall with all those cheap people.

SANJU: All you know is your films.

MANJULA: Thank God! You think I want to be like them? Like your poor little English girl?

Sanju pulls her up out of her chair fiercely.

MANJULA: Yes, go to her! In her nightdress. They have no shame, these women . . .

SANJU: What are you saying!

MANJULA: Everyone knows what they are, these English girls! And today I saw with my own eyes, right on the stage in front of everyone, in a nightdress just like this one.

Sanju crosses the room with her and thrusts her down cruelly on the bed.

SANJU: And what are you? A songstress! You aren't fit to speak her name!

Didiji comes in and hovers protectively over Manjula, who has sprung up into a sitting position. But Sanju is leaving, and Manjula calls after him:

MANJULA: I am Manjula! When I come, hundreds, thousands follow me!

Lizzie's hotel room. She is writing a letter to Sanju in which she intends to break with him once and for all. But it is difficult for her to write it and she keeps scratching out what she has written. Outside, on the dark veranda, we see Sanju making his way towards her room. He searches for her number and finally finds her door. He knocks lightly on the glass.

LIZZIE: Who's there?

SANJU: It's me, Sanju. Let me in.

Lizzie gets up and goes to stand next to the door. Sanju can be seen as a shadowy figure outside. He rattles the doorlatch.

LIZZIE: Go away from the door!

SANJU: It wasn't my fault, I'm ashamed for what she did.

There is a pause and a silence. Lizzie stands uncertain as to what to do. Then she opens the door and Sanju slips inside.

LIZZIE: Come inside, my parents will hear us.

She begins to move away from the door, but immediately he takes her and holds her. She tries to free herself.

SANJU: I never want to see her again.

LIZZIE: You said that the last time.

SANJU: Now it's really true. What do I care for her? She's only an actress.

LIZZIE: That's what I am too.

He now begins to kiss the back of her neck.

SANJU: What?

LIZZIE: An actress.

SANJU: No, you're different. You're Lizzie.

LIZZIE: You always have it your way, don't you. (After a time she says:) Why can't I be angry with you?

SANJU: Because you like me.

She turns round to face him.

LIZZIE: No, because I love you.

He releases her and she walks towards the bed, still holding the writing pad. He follows her. She sits down, carefully pulling her robe together.

LIZZIE: Do you like her very much?

To answer, he sits down next to her and playfully touches her nose. Then he takes her in his arms and begins to kiss her and

caress her. She responds. Suddenly a buzzing sound is heard somewhere and they spring apart. Lizzie puts her hand over Sanju's mouth.

SANJU: What's the matter?

LIZZIE: Shhhh! My parents.

But soon they begin to caress each other again and they lie on the bed.

In the room of Carla and Tony, Tony is doing some accounts before he goes to bed. He looks tired and old. Carla stands before her dressing table and stirs some chocolate she has made. We see Sanju and Lizzie again in the next room. Lizzie looks very happy and at the same time, thoughtful. Their faces are side by side.

The next day. Sanju and Lizzie are amusing themselves in Lizzie's dressing room, trying on bits of costume, ruffs, hats, etc. Sanju is first wearing a bishop's mitre, but Lizzie removes it and ties a ruff round his neck.

SANJU: What this?

LIZZIE: A ruff.

SANJU: Ruff! Ruff!

LIZZIE: You need a moustache.

She draws a moustache on his face. Then she takes some large earrings and tries to put them on him, but he'll have none of this, and he grabs her around the waist and begins to kiss her.

SANJU: Come here, my queen!

Suddenly, they hear approaching footsteps and they spring guiltily apart. It is Carla. She pauses in the doorway. She has not seen them actually kissing each other but she imagines the worst. Sanju is still wearing the false moustache and looks very sheepish.

CARLA: Lizzie! They're waiting for rehearsal.

Lizzie hands Sanju a jar of cold cream, takes her script, and departs, under her mother's disapproving stare.

CARLA: I expect by now you realize what busy lives we lead. Lizzie has no time to play about. Nothing, and nobody must come in the way of her work.

Sanju says nothing. Carla tidies the make-up things and leaves.

CARLA: When you're quite finished, please don't forget to put away all those things.

Sanju sits down at the table after she has left and begins to remove the moustache with cold cream. When he has finished, he flings the cloth onto the table and angrily turns away.

Tony is sorting out some costumes backstage. They are the 18th century things. He is whistling "The British Grenadiers". Lizzie comes up to him, obviously upset and begins to sort out her own things.

TONY: What's the matter?

LIZZIE: Why is Mother so awful to Sanju? She's always telling him off, as if he were a schoolboy of something.

TONY: She wants you to go to England you know.

LIZZIE: That's only to get me away from Sanju.

TONY: Not entirely. She wants you to go to England so you can have all the things she misses so badly herself. She thinks I don't know how homesick she gets . . . I've seen her look at a bloody English postage stamp and burst into tears.

He takes up a tatty bit of costume. Actually it is Bobby's tricorne.

TONY: What a lot of junk!

LIZZIE: We'll have to get some new things.

TONY: Hardly worth it.

LIZZIE: What do you mean?

TONY: I'd been thinking we might go in more for recitals, you know, "Gems from Shakespeare", your mother and I . . . You'd like it in England. Don't you want to see the wide, wide world? Plenty of chances there for a bright girl like you. You've got no spirit of adventure, my dear. You should have seen me at your age . . . Come on, cheer up, the world's not coming to an end.

He puts on a wig and then ties a bow about it in order to amuse her. He begins to sing the British Grenadiers again and she breaks into a smile.

Sanju is sitting alone in one of the boxes in the empty theatre, brooding. A faint sound of hammering comes from backstage. After a moment Lizzie enters behind him and puts her hand over his eyes. He's in no mood for play though and she sits down beside him.

LIZZIE: I'm sorry Mother was so·horrid.

SANJU: It doesn't matter.

LIZZIE: She's always worried about me. She thinks I'll run away, dry up on the stage, get pneumonia.

Sanju begins to relent.

LIZZIE: My father says I'll be just like her when I'm older, so you'd better watch out.

Sanju's face is turned away from her and at this last he stiffens. But Lizzie goes on, touching his hair.

LIZZIE: Why don't you get a haircut?

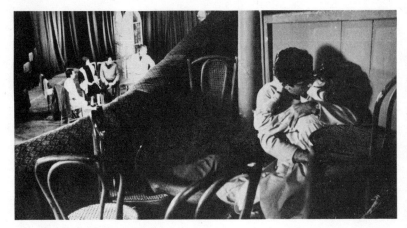

Sanju looks annoyed.

LIZZIE: You know, I was afraid you'd go away and not come back.
Sanju relaxes and kisses her hand which is against his cheek.
We dissolve to another box upstairs in the gallery of the
theatre. Onstage a rehearsal of "School for Scandal" is going on
with Tony, Carla, Aslam and Sharmaji. Their voices come
upstairs very loudly to the upper box, where Lizzie and Sanju
are half-sitting, half-reclining on the floor. They are embracing
passionately. But after a time Sanju pulls away.

LIZZIE: What's the matter?

SANJU: So many people . . .

LIZZIE: It doesn't matter.

They begin again, but again Sanju is distracted.

SANJU: I'd better go.

LIZZIE: Why?

He gets up and goes out. She scrambles up and follows him. On
the stairs going down she asks:

LIZZIE: What's wrong?

SANJU: Nothing.

LIZZIE: Then why are you like that?

SANJU: I'm not used to living in public.

LIZZIE: You'd never make an actor then.

SANJU: No.

LIZZIE: We never have a moment. We even have to dress and undress
in front of everyone . . .

SANJU (stopping and looking at her): Lets not talk about it.

LIZZIE: Don't be so stuffy. Anybody would think I'd done something
wrong.

They are now out in the theatre lobby near the street. Some

teenage boys are lounging there against the door.

LIZZIE: Will I see you tonight?

SANJU: Perhaps.

LIZZIE: What do you mean, perhaps? Good Lord, if you're going to be like that!

FIRST BOY (to LIZZIE): May I have your autograph?

LIZZIE: I don't seem to have anything to write with.

Another boy supplies a pen and she signs. Sanju stands by looking like a stormcloud.

LIZZIE: There, will that do?

One of the boys whispers something to his friend in Hindustani which means "What a doll!" Sanju overhears it and grabs him by the throat.

SANJU: Shut up!

He pushes all three boys down the steps into the street. Lizzie is indignant.

LIZZIE: But they wanted me to sign! I don't understand you.

SANJU: That's a pity.

Sharmaji comes out of the theatre to get Lizzie.

SHARMAJI: Lizzie, your father is shouting!

Without another word Sanju leaves as Lizzie and Sharmaji hurry into the theatre.

Onstage of the theatre. A performance of *Romeo and Juliet* is in progress. Tony is Friar Lawrence, Aslam is Romeo (Act II, Scene 6).

FRIAR LAWRENCE: So smile the heavens upon this holy act

That after hours with sorrow chide us not!

ROMEO: Amen, amen! but come what sorrow can,

FRIAR L: It cannot countervail the exchange of joy
 That one short minute gives me in her sight:
 Do thou but close our hands with holy words,
 Then love-devouring death do what he dare;
 It is enough I may but call her mine.

FRIAR L: These violent delights have violent ends
 And in their triumph die, like fire and powder,
 Which as they kiss consume: the sweetest honey
 Is loathsome in his own deliciousness
 And in the taste confounds the appetite:
 Therefore love moderately; long love doth so;
 Too swift arrives as tardy as too slow.

During the above the camera moves from the stage to the audience. We see Sanju sitting in a box with some of his friends, and in a box next to him, some restless and bored young men. At Lizzie's appearance onstage as Juliet they become excited. One of them whistles. The other members of the audience turn round and tell them to be quiet. One of Sanju's party gives the offending young man a stern look.

FRIAR L: Here comes the lady: O, so light a foot
 Will ne'r wear out the everlasting flint:
 A lover may bestride the gossamer
 That idles in the wanton summer air,
 And yet not fall; so light is vanity.

JULIET: Good even to my ghostly confessor.

FRIAR L: Romeo shall thank thee, daughter, for us both.

JULIET: As much to him, else is his thanks too much.

The noise in the audience increases. There is another whistle, then a sound effect like a falling bomb, loud yawns, and then a cackle like a chicken. Aslam and Lizzie are disturbed onstage but go on as best they can with their lines.

ROMEO: Ah, Juliet, if the measure of thy joy
 Be heap'd like mine and that thy skill be more
 To blazon it, then sweeten with thy breath
 This neighbour air, and let rich music's tongue
 Unfold the imagined happiness that both
 Receive in either by this dear encounter.

JULIET: Conceit, more rich in matter than in words,
 Brags of his substance, not of ornament;
 They are but beggars that can count their worth;
 But my true love is grown to such excess
 I cannot sum up sum of half my wealth.

One of the youths in the box next to Sanju's says something coarse in Punjabi which Sanju understands and which enrages him. In a moment he has jumped into the adjoining box where he knocks one of the boys down. A fight between the occupants of the two boxes starts and the loud noise and commotion alarms the rest of the audience, who, thinking a general riot has broken out, begin making for the exits. But the play continues until the end of the scene:

FRIAR L: Come, come with me, and we will make short work;
    For, by your leaves, you shall not stay alone
    Till holy church incorporate two in one.

Some of the audience run up on the stage to get away from the confusion. The curtain closes and Tony rushes to look out. The fight in the box continues, until Sanju is finally pulled off by his friends. However, the performance is stopped as most of the audience has left.

Backstage later. Sanju and Lizzie are alone. She is bathing his wounds, putting a bandage on the corner of his mouth. But Sanju is still very much worked up.

SANJU: I don't care, I'd do it again. You hear me? Again and again! Standing up there and letting all those goondas whistle at you—Oh, leave it, it's all right!

 He gets up.

LIZZIE: But I'm an actress. I have to be seen . . .

SANJU: By all *those* people. I could have killed him. Do you know what a great-great-grand uncle of mine did? A man had come to the house to sell shawls. He was a stranger, he didn't know our ways. By mistake he went into the women's quarters. My great-uncle seized him by the throat and he *throttled* him! There is an Indian word called —"izzat"—it means, it means honor. When a creature like that whistles at you, it's against *my* izzat, against *my* honour! Do you know what I'm saying?

 Lizzie shakes her head "No". She goes up to him with the wet towel. He avoids her and steps backwards, nearly stumbling over a suitcase of their costumes.

SANJU: Oh, I hate all this! I can't stand the way you live . . .

 He kicks the suitcase and its contents spill out on the floor. Lizzie goes down on her hands and knees to gather them up and faces him in fury:

LIZZIE: You don't know anything about it! I'm proud of what we do, that we're actors, and the company and everything about it! People who've never been on the stage don't know what it's like. It's a wonderful life, I wouldn't want to be anything else. Acting's my whole life . . .

 Here she breaks down and begins to weep. He comes up to her

and lifts her up off her knees.

LIZZIE: Without it I'd be just nothing.

SANJU: I'm sorry I kicked that.

He holds her against him.

LIZZIE: I couldn't give it up. Ever (there is a pause, then . . .) For you I'd give up anything . . . You only have to ask . . .

He hears this, but says nothing. It registers slowly on Lizzie that he has not taken up her offer and she draws back and looks at him. Then she moves away with what dignity she can muster and continues to tidy up their things, putting away the medicine, etc. Sanju begins to button his shirt and put on his coat. She brings him his tie.

LIZZIE: Your collar's torn.

Sanju attempts to touch her nose in the playful gesture he has adopted with her in the past, but she pulls back and walks away.

SANJU: I'll see you tomorrow.

He goes out of the theatre, leaving her alone onstage amidst the trunks and suitcases and pieces of scenery. She sits down on a trunk and begins to gather together some jewellery lying about. After a moment she can't go on, and she breaks down and begins to sob.

Aboard ship. Some weeks later, in Bombay. Lizzie is dressed up for travelling to Europe. Carla and Tony are seeing her off. They sit beside the swimming pool of the first class passengers, waiting for the signal to go ashore. Nobody has much to say. Tony takes a letter out of his pocket and hands it to Lizzie.

TONY: It's from Sharmaji. He asks after you.

She reads it, and smiles.

CARLA: You'll write often, won't you Lizzie?

Lizzie nods, then the announcement, in French and English, for all passengers to go ashore. They get up. Tony hands Lizzie her passport.

TONY: Your passport. Don't lose it. Chin up!

They go out to the gangplank entry, embrace and say farewell in a controlled, English way.

TONY: Goodbye, Lizzie. God bless you. (To the steward): Look after her, will you? She can be a very naughty girl.

Carla and Tony go down the gangplank, leaving Lizzie behind. We see the boat casting off its lines one by one. Tony and Carla are now standing on the dock trying to shout up to Lizzie. The whistle blasts. Carla is making writing motions.

TONY: Don't forget. Write!

LIZZIE: I will.

Lizzie begins to remember Sanju and there is a very short flashback. Lizzie is at the piano in the club at Kalikhet, playing scales. Sanju comes in and stands behind her. He leans over her and plays the Indian equivalent: Sa Re Ga Ma Pa Dha Ni Sa. He makes a rude noise in her ear. We come back to Lizzie aboard the ship. She waves to Carla and Tony. The ship's last line is tossed down. Carla and Tony's figures recede on the dock as Lizzie's does on the ship. The vessel is out in the mainstream now.

THE END